A Sense of Belonging

A Sense of Belonging

Sustaining and Retaining New Teachers

Jennifer Allen

Stenhouse Publishers
Portland, Maine

Stenhouse Publishers
www.stenhouse.com

Library of Congress Cataloging-in-Publication Data
Allen, Jennifer, 1969–
     A sense of belonging : sustaining and retaining new teachers / Jennifer Allen.
     p. cm.
     Includes bibliographical references.
     ISBN 978-1-57110-785-5 (alk. paper)
     1. First year teachers—In-service training—United States. 2. Teachers—Training of—United States. 3. Mentoring in education—United States. I. Title.
     LB2844.1.N4A45 2009
     370.71'55—dc22

                                                          2009019940

Cover design, interior design, and typesetting by Martha Drury
Cover illustration "Confidants" by Deborah DeWit Marchant

Manufactured in the United States of America

PRINTED ON 30% PCW
RECYCLED PAPER

15 14 13 12 11 10 09 9 8 7 6 5 4 3 2 1

To Jessica and Jeni—Our teacher leaders of tomorrow

Contents

Acknowledgments

Ubuntu: *I am because we are.*

<small>THE PHILOSOPHY OF THE SOUTH AFRICAN ZULU TRIBE</small>

This book, like the last, is a reflection of my work, interactions, and collaborations with many educators. I am, because of those who have guided me. I have been mentored by the best. I am forever indebted to those who have taken me under their wings over the years.

For almost the last twenty years I have been learning alongside my colleagues at Waterville (Maine) Public Schools, a district that has promoted lifelong learning and professional learning communities long before they were fashionable. Eric Haley, Peter Thiboutot, Harriet Trafford, Allan Martin, and Barbara Jordan, you are visionary leaders. Janet Morris, thank you for taking me on as a mentee. Teachers of Wing A—Kathleen Ribbons, Lin Fuller, Tina Serdjenian, Sherry Young, Pam Sherbondy, Dottie Megna, Carlene Bickford—you saved me early on as a young teacher. Thank you.

I have had many mentors who have played a part in my educational journey—no mentorship too small. Many probably have no idea of the role they have played in my teaching life. I think back to my first NCTE presentation in Chicago in 1996. As a graduate student, my professor Brenda Power suggested I submit a proposal on my work on literature discussions. She guided me through the unfamiliar application process and continued her support by attending the session. Only ten people (including my mom) attended that presentation. But, at the end of it, Ruth Shagoury approached me and said, "You have got to write that up." Again, I found myself nudged, encouraged, and guided down a new path by a fellow educator, one whom, at the time, I didn't even know. I published my very first article because of that comment. And to top it off, Tom Newkirk, one of the responders at the presentation, praised my work as a classroom teacher. His public words of encouragement validated my risk of sharing my thinking at NCTE, an organization that has fed me professionally for the last twenty years. Tom's handwritten postcard that he sent to my house following the presentation still hangs in my office. One presentation, three people—unbeknownst to them, their words of encouragement set me forth on my educational journey. Thank you. You have taught me that as an educator I too have a responsibility to give back to our profession.

Lindsay Handasyde, thanks for welcoming me into your classroom. You have helped me to remember my own stories as a beginning teacher. We are so lucky to have you as part of our teaching profession. We will be reading about you in years to come.

Philippa Stratton, you are a kind soul and gentle gardener to fragile writers! Your nurturing ways and patience helped me to grow this book. What an honor to work with you and reap the benefits of your brilliant mind.

Brenda Power, you have mentored me from the start. Thank you for seeing something in me when I didn't see it in myself. You have taught me the importance of mentoring others. Thank you for your patience and guidance over the last twenty years. You are a pioneer among educators setting forth new paths of learning for all. Thank you for working with me throughout this book. You supported me when I was ready to give up.

Jay Kilburn, Nate Butler, Bill Varner, Chris Downey, Rebecca Eaton, and everyone at Stenhouse—thank you for your work on the book and for guiding me through the process again.

Martha Drury, you have once again designed a work of art. Thank you.

Leslie Lloyd, thank you for collaborating and implementing with me on new-teacher induction. You have been with this project from the start. You keep me grounded and connected to what is relevant to the classroom. You are a lifelong friend.

Jeni Frazee and Jessica Soucy, thank you for teaching us how to best support new teachers. Your honest input has guided that support. Your optimism and thirst for new learning is contagious. You are both bright stars among educators.

2008/2009 New Teacher Group (Kim, Paula, Uri, and Lindsay), thank you for sharing your thinking and helping us continue to shape new-teacher induction. You have helped us keep the support real and relevant.

Rose Patterson, thank you for being my literacy partner for the last ten years!

Allan Martin, thank you for reading all of my drafts. Your quiet encouragement gently nudged when I didn't think I could write anymore.

Harriet Trafford, thank you for continuing to mentor me. I continue to learn from you.

Liza Finkel, your early reviews and insights helped shape the book.

Cheryl Dozier, thank you for reading my drafts and providing insight when I needed it the most. I wrote with your notes right next to me! Thank you.

Thank you to Franki Sibberson, Joe Mattos, Ann Marie Corgill, Cindy Hatt, Carolyn Bridges, Ralph Fletcher, Lesley Fowler, JoAnn Portalupi, Terry Thompson, Christine Mohlar, Sarah Thibault, Aimee Buckner, Jill Michaud, Ruth Shagoury, Andie Cunningham, Joan Moser, Gail Boushey, Bill Varner—my professional friends who continue to inspire me. Our conversations have pushed my thinking.

Ellie, thank you for teaching me that it is through partnerships that we can overcome roadblocks. You got us to Boston—26.2!

A special wave from the heart to Righteous Red.

Mom, thank you for being my first reader of every draft. Your encouragement and kind words always move me forward even when the writing is less than perfect.

Todd, Ben, and Samantha, thank you for letting me share "our" stories with the teaching world.

I am because we are.

Introduction

We can copy others, we can live to please others, or we can discover that which is unique and precious to us, and paint that, become that.

CARL ROGERS, 1983

I still remember picking up the phone in my kitchen and hearing the words, "We would like to offer you a third-grade position." Eighteen years have passed, yet the call and emotions that filled the moment are still vivid and bring me right back to my start as a classroom teacher, the beginning of my journey as an educator.

As I hung up the phone that day many years ago, I began to dream of my very own classroom. I was ecstatic, ready to take off and face the challenges of classroom teaching. What I lacked in experience, I made up for with enthusiasm and my idealistic vision for creating a community of learners.

I spent the summer gathering resources, prepping materials, and creating the inviting classroom environment that I had envisioned during my days as an undergraduate. I shopped all summer, picking up materials that would stimulate learning. I designed and redesigned the physical layout of my classroom, making sure that I maximized my classroom space. I set out to design a "quality" classroom based on William Glasser's *The Quality School: Managing Students Without Coercion* (1990)—a classroom where students could work together, collaborate, and express themselves freely. I dreamed of a classroom where students would have an opportunity to pursue topics of interest and have a voice in their learning.

I lacked materials—even my flag holder was empty. There were barely enough desks for my students. My classroom library was sparse, but I jazzed it up with a few new titles and borrowed books from the public library. Still, I was not discouraged. Together, the students and I would create a rich learning environment.

September came, the school year was set to start, and I was suddenly panic-stricken. My classroom was set, but I didn't have a clue as to what I should be teaching the first week of school, never mind how I would cover the curriculum over the year. I wasn't even sure how to set up the infrastructure needed for reading and writing workshop.

Then there were the students, all twenty-three of them, including Matthew, a student with autism who had been mainstreamed into my classroom without support. My behavior-management plan based on Glasser's control theory in the classroom (1990) did not prepare me for Matthew and his daily desk-flipping tantrums. To be honest, I wasn't even skilled at controlling the normal chatter level of the classroom. My small repertoire of behavior-management strategies failed me!

I had a mentor assigned to me. She was someone I could turn to with logistical questions about the hot-lunch program, recess, and field trips. She listened to me, but the reality was she was busy teaching all day herself. As a new teacher, I also had to create a teacher action plan, which was a state mandate for acquiring a professional teaching certificate—so unconnected to my immediate needs that I was facing in the classroom.

By October, I was in over my head. It was like I had all the pieces of a puzzle and couldn't put them together. I worked day to day. Every night I planned for the next day, and every Sunday I tried to get ready for Monday. I had no life outside of school.

Days turned to weeks, and the weeks blurred into months. I became disillusioned about my chosen profession, the one I had spent years dreaming about and planning for. I remember walking into the teacher's room one day, so detached. My mentor was there and asked how things were going. I simply responded, "I give myself three years, and then I am out of teaching. I'll start a bakery. I just can't do this."

As I edged toward the end of my first year as a teacher, I felt alone and ineffective. Matthew was becoming more and more disruptive. I was unable to meet his instructional needs, and his behavior was interfering with instructional experiences that I was trying to provide for the rest of the class. Somewhere near the end of the school year, Matthew stood up, flipped his desk, marched toward the exit door of my classroom, and in front of the entire class, pointed his finger at me and declared, "You're fired!" I thought to myself, I wish—someone take me out of my misery!

• • •

Now fast-forward eighteen years. I am no longer a novice classroom teacher, but rather a literacy specialist/coach who has forgotten at times over the years her own story of her first years of teaching.

It took losing several new teachers for me to take a hard look at how we were supporting new teachers within our school. Even though I was supporting them in their classrooms, I knew that they faced many other challenges that we hadn't even begun to touch upon. Struggles in classroom management probably ranked top on this list. In addition, many of our new teachers were scrambling with their day-to-day planning and didn't really have a year-long vision for meeting curricular expectations. There was also no time built into our schedules to meet. I often found myself making quick superficial exchanges with them in the hallway. All their energy went into survival. All my energy went into helping them with the bare essentials of reading and writing workshops. It was clear that these new teachers were not getting the depth and richness of purposeful support that they needed to survive in the classroom.

Katherine, one of the teachers who resigned at the end of her first year, approached me to go over her literacy data. She sat down in frustration and said, "I just don't know if I can do this again." Her response hit me hard. It reminded me of my own first year of teaching—the feelings of despair and disillusionment.

After talking with Katherine and watching other new teachers struggle through their first year, I knew that we were somehow failing them. It was also becoming quite clear to me that beginning teachers enter the profession with a fresh vision and new thinking but often don't get the support they need to put their ideas into practice, as we often overload them with *our* ideas. As a result, we were losing good beginning teachers. Research shows an alarming statistic: "17 percent of educators leave teaching after one year, 30 percent after two years, 40 percent after three years, nearly half after five years, and up to 80 percent after ten years" (Boreen et al. 2000, 6). We were losing good teachers to other professions!

In addition to our inability to retain new teachers in our school, we were losing teachers to retirement. I work in a system with many veteran teachers. Over the next five years, we will lose 27 percent of staff within our district to retirement. With those retirements, we will lose the instructional foundation that we have worked to build as a system unless we find a way to better support beginning teachers. Diane Sweeney, author of *Learning Along the Way*, points out that "constantly integrating new teachers into the school community takes time and energy" (2003, 98). And the reality is that if we fail to provide beginning teachers with the support they need, we will find ourselves in this predicament year after year. Our approach to new-teacher induction had to change. We needed to make sure that our support for new teachers was relevant to their needs. We needed to be more purposeful in how we supported new teachers.

Talking with Lucy

To gain insight into what needed to change, I went to Lucy, a second-year teacher at the time, to get her perspective on new-teacher support. I asked her to talk to me about her needs as a new teacher. Lucy shared with me that she didn't need more information and procedures, but rather craved time to process her thinking with others, solidify classroom structures, and plot out curriculum. She wanted to be able to talk about the obstacles that she faced in the classroom throughout the year without feeling that she was burdening another teacher with her problems. Lucy shared that her mentor and her in-class literacy support were invaluable but that she still could use guidance with implementing curriculum and putting all the pieces together. She told me that she loved the "one" time that she got to observe a colleague's literacy block and went on to say that she was learning so much from the teacher next to her and would love more opportunities to watch other teachers in action with students. For Lucy, one of the highlights of being a new teacher was her participation in literacy study groups. She talked about how she loved participating in the groups and the sense of belonging that was generated through them.

After listening to Lucy share her struggles of being a new teacher, I shared a reflection I'd written about my first year of teaching (what is now the beginning of this book), describing my feelings of isolation and struggles with classroom management. When she finished reading it, Lucy said that she could identify with all of my emotions and went on to say, "It's still really hard for me to reflect and think about my first year of teaching." I replied, "It took me fifteen years to put my beginning teaching experience on paper." Writing about my experience as a new teacher made the issue regarding lack of teacher support all too real to ignore.

Rethinking New-Teacher Support

Harry Wong writes that effective induction programs for new teachers have three basic components. They are comprehensive, coherent, and sustained (Wong 2005). Although we had support systems in place I am not sure that they were comprehensive, coherent, or sustained. It was as if our supports were offered in isolation of one another.

We had been offering support to new teachers but were not providing repeated opportunities over time with scaffolds in place to help them integrate their new learning. Coaching new teachers in their classrooms once a week was just not enough. I also knew that the support for new teachers needed to extend beyond their first year of teaching and that somehow we needed to provide the same elements of gradual release that we provide our students to help them sustain new practices. I thought about my conversation with Lucy and the elements of support that she craved in addition to the existing support and generated a list of wonderings.

New Wonderings

- How could we provide new teachers from the start with a sense of belonging?
- How do we build in time within the school day for new teachers to collaborate and learn from one another?
- How do we provide ongoing opportunities for new teachers to observe other teachers in action?
- How could we help new teachers see how student assessments are part of what we do rather than an add-on?
- How could we support new teachers in using student work on a day-to-day basis to inform their instruction?
- How could we support new teachers with curriculum planning so that they embrace the planning process as a continuous cycle?
- How do we support new teachers so that they can become the teacher they want to be and at the same time maintain consistency in the delivery of district curriculum?
- How do we retain new, smart, innovative teachers in this challenging field of education?
- How do we figure out what makes a difference?

Our Comprehensive New-Teacher Induction

The list of wonderings that I generated from my conversation with Lucy guided my thinking as we reorganized new-teacher induction.

So what changed? We reflected on existing resources and became smarter and more systematic in how we supported teachers. We shifted from a hit-or-miss model of support to a systematic new-teacher induction model that has new teachers working together through their challenges, month after month over the course of two years.

We also rethought our definition of what it means to be a new teacher. We now define a beginning teacher as anyone within their first three years of teaching. Research shows "a one-to-two-year period of induction can make the difference between a teacher who succeeds early in their career and one who does not, and between a teacher who remains in the profession and one who does not. Too brief, and the program may have little more impact than a stint of student teaching" (Wiebke and Bardin 2009, 34). We also include teachers who may be considered veteran, but who are new to our system in new-teacher induction.

Support for New Teachers

- **Human Resources**
  As a literacy coach, I am one of many human resources for new teachers within the school. We work to develop relationships with them prior to the start of the school year. We believe that a sense of trust needs to be established before we tackle curriculum.

- **Monthly New-Teacher Group Meeting**
  This is a monthly release day for new teachers. This layer of support provides new teachers with time built into their school day to get together with the other new teachers in the school.

- **Support Administering and Analyzing District Assessments**
  Over the course of the year we work with new teachers to administer and analyze assessments to students. We plot out assessment schedules, work together to administer the assessments, and take time to analyze the assessments together. We look at how the information from the assessments informs instruction.

- **In-Class Support for Reading and Writing Workshop**
  As a literacy coach I support new teachers in the classroom for reading and writing. I work in a first-year teacher's classroom three times a week for at least forty-five minutes and continue to support them in their second and third year at least once a week or as needed.

- **Peer Observations**
  Peer observations are built into the morning of the monthly release day for new teachers. New teachers spend the morning observing their

peers and then meet as a group and debrief the observations during the afternoon.

- **Using Student Work to Guide Instruction**
  Student work is incorporated into new-teacher group meetings. We use student work to reflect on student progress around targeted learning goals and to inform instruction and adjust our teaching accordingly.
- **Curriculum Planning**
  New teachers are supported in curriculum planning. Time is designated during the afternoon of each monthly group meeting to explore, learn, and make sense of curriculum. Mentors also support new teachers with curriculum.
- **Study Groups**
  New teachers are invited and encouraged to participate in voluntary professional study groups on a chosen topic. These groups provide a more informal opportunity for new teachers to share their professional thinking, collaborate with their peers, and pursue learning together.
- **Mentors**
  Each new teacher is assigned a teacher mentor within the district. This is state-mandated support for new teachers with a conditional certificate in their first two years of teaching. We work with the mentor so that the support the mentor provides is coordinated with all the other support the new teacher receives.

Frequent, Intensive, Individualized Support

New teachers in our school are now part of what Harry Wong would identify as a comprehensive, coherent, and sustained new-teacher induction program. The support we give them is designed to provide frequent but varied opportunities for learning. Curt Dudley-Marling and Patricia Paugh write that struggling readers benefit from frequent, intensive, and individualized instruction (2004). We believe that beginning teachers will also benefit from a framework of support that is frequent, intensive, and individualized. It is our responsibility to provide meaningful professional development opportunities and support for new educators—opportunities and support that are relevant and connected to the day-to-day challenges that teachers face in the classroom. It is important that the support we provide to new teachers is designed to sustain itself over time—ultimately fostering a culture of lifelong learning.

Our Hope

If we invest in beginning teachers up front and provide them with more support in the beginning of their teaching career, then we will reap the pay-off in the long run—skilled, thoughtful, reflective, and energized educators who are essential members within our collaborative learning community and committed to student learning and achievement.

There is also evidence that induction programs save money. Estimates figure that for every $1.00 invested, there is a return of $1.66 after five years (Moir 2008). And with teacher retirements in our future, and the incorporation of new teachers within our system, we needed to protect our investment in new teachers!

Today

Here I am, almost twenty years after my start as a classroom teacher, working as a literacy specialist/coach supporting new teachers in our district in the small city of Waterville, Maine. The free- and reduced-lunch population is about 56 percent, and we have a yearly transient rate of 33 percent. Students come and go and come back. I work with students and teachers in grades three through five at the George J. Mitchell School (grade three) and the Albert S. Hall School (grades four and five).

Over the years I have been able to recapture my enthusiasm for the profession and remain passionate about learning and supporting others in their personal learning journey. But I have never truly forgotten my first year. My own story as a beginning teacher now guides me as I work to support new teachers in the challenges that they face.

In *The Energy to Teach*, Donald Graves writes, "Finally, we have to remember that when confronted by a world and profession that is in a hurry to get to an unknown destination, that we relax, listen carefully, become informed and ask tough, persistent questions. We relax because we know that we are on a long journey on behalf of our children" (2001, 98). Donald Graves reminds me that learning is a journey, and that we need to slow down and provide meaningful and relevant support to new teachers so that we can keep positive energy flowing within our schools. And it is our hope that we can all learn to catch some of the contagious enthusiasm, fresh thinking, and limitless energy that new teachers bring to our profession.

CHAPTER ONE

Relationships

The nature of relationships among the adults within a school has a greater influence on the character and quality of that school and on student accomplishment than anything else.

Roland Barth, 2006

Feeling alone and uncomfortable at the inservice breakfast. That is what I remember about my first official day as a new teacher. I vividly remember walking into the cafeteria and nervously searching for a familiar face. I didn't know anyone, so I am not exactly sure who I was looking for. Walking into this mob of strangers was so uncomfortable. I don't even know where I ended up sitting. I just found an empty seat and sat down as other teachers chatted on about their summer—no one even pausing to see who had joined their table.

From breakfast everyone migrated into the high school auditorium. My first morning on the job went from bad to worse when the superintendent called new staff members down front to the stage and introduced us individually.

I was mortified. My first day was filled with awkward and uncomfortable situations with adults whom I didn't even know. The sense of feeling alone continued beyond that first day. In fact, I felt alone for the first two years of teaching. Even though there were seven other teachers on the third-grade team, I never saw them except for staff and team meetings, meetings that were typically all about budgets, assemblies, and field trips.

At the end of my second year of teaching, just about the time that I thought I would leave the profession forever, I was asked by a group of teachers if I would be interested in creating a school within a school. The idea was that we would work together to create a community of learners (kindergartners through third graders) within one of the wings of our school.

It was after this invitation that I started collaborating and planning with colleagues. There was a huge sense of community and a sense that we were in this together. I also found colleagues with similar philosophical beliefs about students and learning. It was the first time that I felt that I belonged, and I found myself getting excited about teaching. I hadn't felt this way since the summer before I started teaching. Finally, I had colleagues off of whom I could bounce ideas and who would help me sort out new thinking.

It was the first time within the large school that I didn't feel so alone. I know the students benefited from this collaborative endeavor, but I think the reality is that Wing A saved me as a teacher.

Over time, I found my niche as a classroom teacher and, later, literacy coach. But unfortunately, with time, I had forgotten not only my own stories but my life lessons of being a new teacher.

I admit that as a new literacy coach I got caught up with district literacy expectations and all that I thought new teachers "needed." Although I was striving to support the new staff, I somehow had overlooked Maslow's hierarchy of needs—that being a sense of belonging, the very thing I had craved as a new teacher myself (Maslow 1943). And it took a new teacher to remind me of the importance of relationships.

Fostering Relationships with New Teachers

A few years ago I received an e-mail at home from Jessica, a newly hired fourth-grade teacher, in mid-July prior to the start of school. I could sense her energy through the cable line. Jess had just finished setting up her classroom, and she was thrilled with the layout; her desks were in groups and there were enough chairs for all her students. She was especially proud to share about her classroom library and how she had organized the books, many of which she had bought on eBay. Jess also shared her thoughts on the professional reading she had done over the summer. She had enjoyed

Nonfiction Craft Lessons by Ralph Fletcher and JoAnn Portalupi (2001) and now planned to incorporate nonfiction into both her reading and writing workshops. She had even started designing a layered nonfiction unit on Egyptian mummies to kick off the year in hopes that the high-interest topic would engage students. So many ideas to try out in the classroom! She reminded me of myself years ago, my first summer of nesting prior to my students' arrival. I immediately e-mailed Jess back in support of all of her thinking and new ideas. In Jessica, I saw an opportunity to refine my work with new teachers in hopes of providing the right balance of support for success on that personal journey.

Then, about two weeks before school I got another note from Jess. This one was different—full of fear. The gist of it was that she was petrified of starting the school year and was having nightmares. Visions of out-of-control students filled her dreams at night.

Jess and I met the following week for lunch. We talked for over two hours and laughed off the vision of a room full of fourth graders ruling the classroom. Again she shared all of her brilliant, thoughtful ideas about starting the school year, right down to her behavior-management system. Her excitement and energy was contagious—I found myself secretly wishing I was back teaching in the classroom!

Halfway through lunch I finally asked, "Why are you so petrified?" She told me that now that her classroom environment was set up, her fears of not knowing what to do were settling in. We talked about what the first day of school might look like and the importance of routines and a predictable schedule from day one. I asked a lot of questions and did a lot of listening. I also told her if she wasn't anxious and nervous about the beginning of school, I would be worried about her. What educator is not nervous about the start of the school year? I know my own nervous energy starts to kick in by the beginning of August. Jessica's fears of not knowing what she was going to be teaching, losing control to the kids, and establishing routines are really universal fears for new teachers, issues that we begin to address at the start, and even before the start, of school.

Initiating the Teacher/Coach Relationship

This learning experience with Jessica led me to start sending cards out to new teachers at the beginning of August letting them know my role as literacy coach (see Figure 1.1). I always include contact information so that they can get in touch with me with questions or requests for resources as

---

SAMPLE WELCOME CARD

Dear Christine,

Welcome to our school! We are lucky to have you join our staff. I hope you are enjoying a restful summer and taking advantage of the warm weather.

I wanted to introduce myself. I work as the literacy coach/specialist in the school. Part of my role is to support you as a new teacher. Please feel free to call or e-mail me if you have any questions or just want to touch base as you think ahead to the start of school!

We offer many study groups at the school. They provide a great opportunity to get to know your colleagues and explore a topic of interest. One is on designing learning environments and will be held before the start of school on the morning of August 22. We would love to have you join us. Let me know if this is of interest to you, and I can sign you up and fill you in on the details.

Enjoy the rest of your summer,
      Jen

Figure 1.1

they think ahead to the upcoming school year. That first card mailed to new staff is my way of reaching out. It is a small, cordial gesture letting them know that they are welcome additions to our school.

This year all of the new staff responded right back to me. Several e-mailed to thank me for the card and included questions; others called to talk and process their ideas for the start of school. The simple act of sending home the cards opened our door to communication.

Summer Study Group: An Opportunity to Meet Colleagues

A few years ago I started offering a two-hour study-group session on designing learning environments the week before school started. It was intended to be a reflective jump-start session for the upcoming year and was for all teachers (new and existing). (See Figure 1.2 for the agenda.)

In her book *Teaching with Intention: Defining Beliefs, Aligning Practice, Taking Action, K–5*, Debbie Miller (2008) encourages teachers to think about what they value about teaching and learning as they set up their classrooms for the year. My study-group session gives staff a chance to reconnect from the summer and, at the same time, a chance to examine their classroom design to see if it reflects their educational beliefs about learning. And for new teachers, it provides a small-group informal setting

AGENDA: DESIGNING LEARNING ENVIRONMENTS

Self-Reflection (15 minutes)
- What are my beliefs about a learning environment?
- How will these be reflected in my room?

Read (15 minutes)
- "Establishing an Environment for Learning" (Boushey and Moser 2006a)

Discussion (15 minutes)

Video Viewing (30 minutes)
- View excerpts from the videotape *Simply Beautiful: Classroom Design for Gracious Living* (Boushey and Moser 2006c)
- Two-column notes: What I would like to try / Potential roadblocks
   —Model classroom tour   —Children's artwork
   —Lighting   —Storage area
   —Meeting area

Read/Discussion (15 minutes)
- "Seven Steps: Designing the Physical Space" (Boushey and Moser 2006b)
- Choose one of the following photo essays by The Sisters to read
   —Personal Touches Early in the Year
   —Tight Spaces: Maximizing Room for Literacy Learning
   —Wall Displays
- Sketch
   —Sketch out classroom design

Video Viewing (15 minutes)
- View excerpts of Franki Sibberson's classroom from *Bringing Reading to Life*
- Two-column notes: What I would like to try / Potential roadblocks

Putting Ideas into Practice (15 minutes)
- What might you try?
- What are your next steps?

Resources:
- Boushey, Gail, and Joan Moser. 2006. *Simply Beautiful: Classroom Design for Gracious Living and Learning* [DVD]. Holden, ME: Choice Literacy Productions.
- Sibberson, Franki, and Karen Szymusiak. 2003. *Still Learning to Read: Teaching Students in Grades 3–6*. Portland, ME: Stenhouse.
- Articles from Choice Literacy Web site, www.choiceliteracy.com

Figure 1.2

where they can connect with colleagues, reflect on their beliefs, and gather fresh ideas on classroom design. The topic of designing learning environments is especially appealing to new teachers since it is relevant to their immediate needs.

An added bonus for participants is a fifty-dollar purchase order so that they can buy something of their choice that will enhance their classroom environment. This gives new teachers some monetary support to purchase an added resource that they may be lacking or a chance to implement a new idea. This year, teachers chose a range of resources, including items such as a fan (this teacher was on the third floor), a metal storage unit, book bins for the classroom library, plastic storage containers for community supplies, pillows for the reading area, and hanging files and a storage case for student writing.

As a literacy coach, I was able to see immediate transfer and application of ideas gathered from the study group and incorporated into their rooms. Many of the new teachers asked me to stop by their classroom to view the changes they had made in response to participating in the group. Often they pointed out a particular area to me. One teacher wanted to share how she purchased hanging file folders and a crate to organize student writing. Another teacher wanted to show off her classroom library and how she redesigned it using tips that she learned from watching the video excerpt from *Simply Beautiful* by The Sisters (Boushey and Moser 2006) that we had just viewed in the study group. The power of having the new teachers participate in this group wasn't so much about classroom design, but rather it was the networking and cultivation of relationships between new and veteran staff.

First Few Weeks of School

The first few weeks of interacting with new teachers are just like the first few weeks of interacting with students as a classroom teacher. It is a time to get to know them as individuals. I observe, listen, and get a sense of the type of classroom teachers hope to create so that I can best support them during the year. I strive to differentiate my support to match their individual needs as learners just as classroom teachers want to tailor instruction for their students.

I have unique conversations with each new teacher depending on his or her needs. Conversations often take us in different directions, and I find

EXAMPLES OF SUPPORTING NEW TEACHERS PRIOR TO THE START OF SCHOOL

Teachers	Visit #1	Visit #2	Visit #3	Visit #4
Christine Came to see me before the start of summer while school was still in session.	She was hired before the end of the school year and has a preschool background. When she asked me for a professional book to read over the summer, I recommended *Still Learning to Read* (Sibberson and Szymusiak 2003) and also gave her the Literacy Notebook to browse through.	I approached her and asked to meet to get a sense of the support that she would need for fall assessments. She shared that she did not have experience in administering them. I could sense that she was overwhelmed and tried to assure her that we would get through this together and not worry about it for now.	Met again to talk about fall literacy expectations. We picked two release days and arranged for substitutes so that we could work together on administering the Developmental Reading Inventory (DRA) to her students. We plotted out a strategy of fitting in the fall assessments.	We worked on her daily schedule; she was trying to fit in all of her literacy requirements and specifically wanted advice on where she should fit word study into her day.
Katie E-mailed me as soon as she received the card I had sent at the beginning of August.	She participated in the study group on Learning Environments, where she brainstormed organizational ideas for storing student writing. In the end she came up with the idea of hanging file folders.	I was invited into the classroom to see how she organized student writing folders and her writing workshop area.	She wanted to start the year with a whole-class read, and we brainstormed possible books that she could use with her fifth-grade class. She specifically wanted a book that would be accessible to most students but one that would be high interest and engaging. In the end she decided on *Sideways Stories from Wayside School* by Louis Sachar (1985) and used budget money to purchase a classroom quantity of books.	Met again to talk about fall literacy expectations. I gave her the Literacy Notebook. We sketched out a plan on how we would administer fall assessments and talked about how I would support her through the process. She had prior experience with the DRA but welcomed support with the first few students.

(continued on next page)

Figure 1.3

myself supporting each of them differently based on those conversations (see Figure 1.3). Early support may range from helping a new teacher organize the classroom library to helping him or her become more familiar with district assessment materials.

EXAMPLES OF SUPPORTING NEW TEACHERS PRIOR TO THE START OF SCHOOL

Teachers	Visit #1	Visit #2	Visit #3	Visit #4
Edward Called me in late August to talk about grade-level expectations and what he himself could expect the first year. Wanted to make sure that his thinking matched the school's thinking.	He participated in the study group on Learning Environments. He really wanted to work on organization of his classroom library.	Invited me into the room to view his library. He used the money from the study group to buy bins to organize books. He also purchased a rug with his own money and placed it in the library and made a reading corner for his students.	In talking about his library, he still wished he had a few more books that were newer and might engage students. He was specifically interested in gathering more series books that might grab his students and be accessible to his lower-level readers. He wanted to get input from his students on the types of books they would like for their classroom library. I told him that I could give him 2,000 bonus points to purchase series books from the catalogs. When school began, he had his students choose books from the catalogs and involved them in the process.	I asked him to meet with me to talk about fall assessments to get a sense of his background in administering literacy assessments. He was unfamiliar with them. I scheduled time within my calendar to make sure that I would be available to support him with his fall assessments, and we also sketched out a plan on how we would fit them in.

Figure 1.3
(continued)

Life Lessons from Jessica

My interactions and informal conversations with Jessica that summer a few years ago reminded me of the importance of making connections and fostering relationships. I realized that the most important resource that I could provide for new staff was reaching out to them and being available to listen. I discovered that I didn't have to wait until the start of a school year. As a teacher, I never waited for the first day of school to get to know my incoming students. I always started my summer by sending out post-cards to them, encouraging them to write to me throughout the summer.

The same can be done to start building relationships with new staff—through e-mails, phone calls, and notes as soon as individuals are hired. As a literacy coach working to support new teachers and staff, I saw how I could take advantage of the summer months to start fostering these relationships and share materials. I believe coaching/mentoring works best if there is a trusting relationship between the coach and the teacher. I have learned that being a resource is just as important—if not more so—as providing resources.

CHAPTER TWO

Observing the Coach

There are three principal means of acquiring knowledge . . .
observation of nature, reflection, and experimentation.
Observation collects facts; reflection combines them;
experimentation verifies the result of that combination.

DENIS DIDEROT

As a first-year teacher in 1991, I was formally observed three times throughout the year. The image is still vivid of Nancy, my principal, coming into my room with her yellow legal pad and taking a seat on the outer edge of the classroom. She sat taking notes, scripting my every word.

I always stressed preparing for the observation. I often ditched my original plan for the day and would spend hours just thinking up that perfect lesson, which I have to admit at times was completely unconnected to what we were learning about. I remember trying to fit all of Madeline Hunter's (1982) components of a lesson—often referred to as the Madeline Hunter Model—into my forty-five-minute observation. I knew it might be the only time I had to demonstrate my competency to any adult until the next time I was observed, and that would be at least a month or two down the road; by then we would have moved on to a different unit. As a new teacher I viewed observations as isolated, performance-like events in which I aimed to showcase lessons for my administrator. I put all my energy into the execution of the lesson and spent little time reflecting on and noticing whether students had actually learned what I thought I was teaching. I equated strong observations with being an effective teacher and didn't realize that being effective is really about knowing your students and adjusting daily plans to meet their needs.

I would always breathe a sigh of relief at the end of the observation when Nancy would pick up her pad and exit the classroom. She would always leave silently, never saying a word. She was there and then she was gone. And then I would begin my obsessing over the observation: what I could have done differently, what Nancy might have thought of "the lesson." Because all that really mattered to me was that Nancy liked it.

I would then wait. Wait for a note in my mailbox from Nancy giving me a day and time for when she could go over her observation of me.

"Stance and Dance"

When I became a coach I realized that I didn't want to replicate the observations I had endured as a new teacher, yet I wasn't sure how to do it differently. I didn't want to make the teacher uncomfortable so I always sat at the back of the classroom, taking minimal notes and focusing my observations on the students rather than on the teacher. But what I realized was that just my being there in the classroom was intimidating to new teachers. No matter how hard I tried to slink into the background my presence was still known and they still perceived that I was watching and judging them. One teacher, Lucy, would come up to me at the end of every lesson and ask me what I thought of it. So I began to wonder if sitting back and observing at the beginning of the year was really the best way to foster sustainable, trusting, professional relationships with new teachers and at the same time get at the heart of instruction.

I remember the exact moment that my vision for observations and coaching began to come together. I was sitting in a crammed room of educators at an NCTE session, overheating. As uncomfortable as I was, I wish I could have bottled the inspiration I felt at that particular session as I listened to Bruce Morgan, Debbie Miller, and Ellin Keene speak about personal learning experiences that made a significant impact on them as educators. Bruce and Debbie said that as classroom teachers their most powerful personal experiences were those in which they had opportunities to reflect and dialogue on their instructional practices with colleagues. Ellin Keene added that the professional learning experiences that are most successful have a "spirit of experimentation." I was reminded of a quote by Stephen Brookfield from his book *Becoming a Critically Reflective Teacher*: "Critical reflection is a matter of stance and dance. Our stance is one of inquiry. We see it as a constant formation and always needing further investigation. Our dance is the dance of experimentation and risk" (1995, 42). That was it! That was what I was after! I needed to reverse the roles. Rather than me observing them, I wanted new teachers to have the opportunity to observe my "stance and dance." I wanted them to embrace a spirit of experimentation and, at the same time, have ongoing opportunities to talk about what they observed and share new thinking as they set out on the beginning of their educational journey.

Pinnell and Rodgers point out, "Effective teachers observe students closely and make constant adjustments to their teaching to support learning" (2004, 171). This was what I wanted our new teachers to see, so I invited them to observe and take notes on me as I led demonstration lessons in their classrooms. I wanted new teachers to see my own reflective process as I worked through some of the very challenges (especially in the area of classroom management) that they faced in their classrooms. I wanted them to see that teaching never becomes "easy," that as a veteran teacher I am constantly reflecting and adjusting lessons to meet the needs of students, and that I too sometimes struggle with what to do. Recently, I had a student stretch out on the floor during the middle of class and refuse to work (I kid you not), and I failed miserably to motivate her as the teacher looked on with a smirk. Ultimately, I want new teachers to see how they could acquire knowledge through observation, reflection, and experimentation.

Taking Notes on Me

With first-year teachers, I am usually in their classrooms for reading or writing workshop offering support three days a week from September through April. This schedule is sustained day to day, week to week throughout the year. For the first half of the year, I lead demonstration lessons to give new teachers an opportunity to observe me and take notes. The frequency with which I am in their classrooms modeling lessons also increases their comfort level with me and promotes a collaborative environment. (See the sample schedule shown in Figure 2.1.)

As the year progresses, I continue to work in a first-year teacher's room three times a week for in-class support but will tend to reduce demonstra-

SAMPLE WEEKLY SCHEDULE OF IN-CLASS SUPPORT FOR JESSICA: SEPTEMBER

Monday	Tuesday	Wednesday	Thursday	Friday
9:30–10:15 Writing Workshop (In-class support)	9:30–10:15 Writing Workshop (In-class support)	9:30–10:15 Writing Workshop (In-class support)	9:30–10:15 Writing Workshop (Independent)	9:30–10:15 Writing Workshop (Independent)
I lead the lesson.	I lead the lesson.	I lead the lesson.	Jessica leads the lesson.	Jessica leads the lesson.
We always do a quick debrief at the end of the lesson.			Meet with Jessica during prep period for planning.	

Figure 2.1

tion lessons down to once or twice a week. (See Figure 2.2.) It's a truly collaborative process of demonstrating and then gradually letting go as the teacher comes to know the norms, routines, and expectations for writing workshop, and together we come to know the strengths and quirks of individual students in the class in a way that I couldn't if I was just observing.

Figure 2.2

SAMPLE WEEKLY SCHEDULE OF IN-CLASS SUPPORT FOR JESSICA: FEBRUARY

Monday	Tuesday	Wednesday	Thursday	Friday
9:30–10:15 Writing Workshop (In-class support)	9:30–10:15 Writing Workshop (In-class support)	9:30–10:15 Writing Workshop (In-class support)	9:30–10:15 Writing Workshop (Independent)	9:30–10:15 Writing Workshop (Independent)
I lead the lesson.	Jessica leads the lesson.	Jessica leads the lesson.	Jessica leads the lesson.	Jessica leads the lesson.
			Meet with Jessica during prep period for debriefing and planning.	

When new teachers observe me leading a demonstration lesson, I invite them to use an Observation Notes form (Figure 2.3; also in appendix) or a Two-Column Notes form (Figure 2.4; also in appendix) to capture their observations. These tools help teachers focus their viewing and also serve as a vehicle to launch our lesson debrief. The Observation Notes form outlines various components of a lesson. It has the observer zoom in on what the teacher is doing; what students are doing; evidence of gradual release;

Figure 2.3

OBSERVATION NOTES FORM

Teacher: _____   Date: _____
Sketch the room on the back.

Focus of Lesson:

Zone in On . . .	Distribution of Time	What Do You Notice?	What Do You Wonder?	What Might You Like to Try?
Teacher (What is the teacher doing?)				
Evidence of Gradual Release				
Student Engagement (What are the students doing?)				
Materials				
Environment				
Assessment (How do you know the students are getting it?)				

TWO-COLUMN NOTES FORM

What I Notice	What I Might Try in My Classroom

Figure 2.4

materials; environment; and, most importantly, assessment—how do you know the students are getting it? I also want teachers to look at the distribution of time. Did they observe a mini-lesson? How long is a mini-lesson? The expectation is not to fill out every block of the organizer but to focus their viewing. The goal of both forms is to help new teachers observe and reflect on important parts of instruction. By doing so, they can start to look for those aspects of instruction in themselves. Having new teachers take notes on me with these organizers also gives them an opportunity to become familiar with the forms, since they are the same ones used for peer observations. (See Chapter 6 for more on peer observations.) The forms for demonstration lessons are used only in the beginning of the year and, as new teachers feel more comfortable, are replaced by the teachers' own notes often written down on a piece of paper or in a journal.

During my lessons I model child-watching strategies and demonstrate how I gather information in regard to student learning in the midst of lessons. I do this by taking anecdotal notes on students during the lesson. What is it that I notice students are doing? What evidence do I see that students are getting the lesson? I look for the students who need reteaching and identify those who are ready to move on. I try to emphasize to new teachers the importance of focusing as much on what students are doing as on what the teacher is doing.

Knowing the importance of timely feedback, I engage in a short debrief with teachers at the end of lessons as students work independently. The purpose of the debriefs is both to capture our observations right then and there so that they are not forgotten and to promote reflection, allowing new teachers to see how we can adjust and tweak lessons on a day-to-day basis to better meet the needs of the class.

Observing the Coach: Year One

One of our new fourth-grade teachers, Christine, embraced the opportunity to take notes on me as we worked to launch her writing workshop. Our plan was that I would lead the writing workshop lessons, three times a week, for the first part of the year. Christine and I met during one of her prep periods every week for additional debriefs and planning.

Although supporting Christine by demonstrating in her room is important, it is only part of a larger pattern of support and communication (see Figure 2.5).

Christine had a tough class, full of challenging student behaviors. I had already experienced one of her students; the girl who had decided to sprawl out on the floor was from her room. She was happy to hand over writing workshop and see how I would handle the various behaviors. I think she wanted me to see just how difficult it was for her to get through instruction when five of her students wreaked havoc on a daily basis within the room by such behaviors as refusing to work, ripping up paper, calling out, and simply getting up and walking out of the room while she was trying to instruct.

So began my teaching in Christine's room. During one of my initial demonstration lessons, I introduced the strategy of sketching a setting map to generate story titles, an idea I had gotten from Ralph Fletcher's book *How to Write Your Life Story* (2007). To be honest, one of my primary goals of the lesson was to engage the students. I knew from being in the classroom and talking with Christine that many of them were not fond of writing and that she was having a hard time motivating them. I was hoping that by having the students sketch out and talk about their ideas with their classmates, they would be more receptive to writing workshop and would see that there was more to writing than just writing.

Christine immediately noticed the amount of productive talk throughout the classroom. She zoomed in on time distribution and saw that students had chunks of time to share their maps and talk about their ideas. She

A Month's Overview of Support for Christine: October

Monday	Tuesday	Wednesday	Thursday	Friday
		1 In-class support 8:30–9:15	**2** New-teacher meeting Peer observations Afternoon study-group assessment 3:00	**3** District inservice
In-class support 8:30–9:15 Meet 1:45–2:15 with Christine	Full-day release to work with Christine on reviewing student assessments			
6 In-class support 8:30–9:15 Meet 1:45–2:15 with Christine	**7** In-class support 8:30–9:15	**8** In-class support 8:30–9:15	**9**	**10** Student literacy data due
13 Columbus Day No school	**14** In-class support 8:30–9:15 Meet 1:45–2:15 with Christine	**15** In-class support 8:30–9:15	**16**	**17**
20 In-class support 8:30–9:15 Meet 1:45–2:15 with Christine Staff meeting	**21** In-class support 8:30–9:15	**22** In-class support 8:30–9:15	**23**	**24** Family Literacy Breakfast Lynn Plourde *Margaret Chase Smith: A Woman for President*
27 Morning Study Group Children's Lit 7:15 In-class support 8:30–9:15	**28** In-class support 8:30–9:15	**29** In-class support 8:30–9:15	**30**	**31**

Figure 2.5

also noticed that I embedded "turn and talk" throughout the writing workshop. Turn and talk is when you periodically stop the whole group and have students turn to the person next to them and share their thinking. The purpose of this strategy is "to process information, to enhance understanding, and to maximize engagement" (Harvey and Goudvis 2007, 54). Christine thought it was an effective strategy for engaging her students.

As I noticed students generating titles, I would put a plus sign next to those titles on their maps, giving kids immediate feedback. Christine picked up on the fact that her students were highly motivated by this simple mark. Some students were even raising their hand so that I could go back and give them another plus mark as they generated more titles. Christine wanted to know more about this strategy since it seemed to have a positive effect on her students.

Although most of the students were drawing and generating possible story titles, I still had a few who were waiting me out, and Christine watched on as I tried to motivate the ones who were not producing. Trez was one of those students. He had virtually nothing on his paper but a very rudimentary drawing of a house (Figure 2.6). When I asked him about his drawing, he told me that he didn't like to write or draw. Although he was reluctant to write, he wanted a plus on his paper. I prompted him to tell me about his map, and he said that he liked to ride his bike around the block. I then wrote this on his map and walked away. What I noticed next was that Trez started adding to his map and then independently wrote "Ride bike around the block" as his first title on his title list. This was a huge step since he had basically withdrawn from the activity and was sitting at his desk playing with a variety of pencils. At the end of class Trez actually came up to me and asked if I would put his work on an overhead so that he could share his thinking with the class the next day.

Christine observed that I checked in with all of the students and made sure that every child had at least one title before the end of writing

Figure 2.6
Trez's Map
and Titles

WRITING WORKSHOP—STRATEGIES FOR GENERATING IDEAS

*White areas indicate days I will come and lead the lesson.

Monday

Mentor Text:	*Marshfield Dreams* by Ralph Fletcher ("Jimmy"); share map from *Marshfield Dreams*, and share my map from home in Vermont **Basic Story Ingredients (Plot, Character, Setting)**
Strategy:	Sketching Out a Setting
Share:	Sketches

Tuesday: Generating Ideas/Finding Our Stories

Mentor Text:	The poem "Valentine for Ernest Mann" by Naomi Shihab Nye **Review Basic Story Ingredients (Plot, Character, Setting)**
Strategy:	Sketching Out a Setting (finish)
Writer's Notebook:	Generate at least four titles for your writer's notebook
Share:	Titles (five minutes)

Wednesday

Mentor Text:	*Grandpa Never Lies* by Ralph Fletcher **Review Basic Story Ingredients (Plot, Character, Setting)**
Strategy:	Heart Map (Special People and Stories)
Writer's Notebook:	Generate at least four titles for your writer's notebook
Share:	Titles

*Homework: Pass out paper lunch bags; have students bring in three special objects that fit in the bag.

Thursday

Mentor Text:	*The Keeping Quilt* by Patricia Polacco **Review Basic Story Ingredients (Plot, Character, Setting)**
Strategy:	Personal Artifacts (Special Objects and the Stories Behind Them)
Model:	Using one of your personal objects
Writer's Notebook:	Generate at least four titles for your writer's notebook; circle the title off of the title page that will be your first story.
Share:	Writing on the object

Friday

Mentor Text:	"George" (Teacher Story)
Writer's Notebook:	Start drafting first story
Share:	Student comments and compliments (five minutes)

Figure 2.7 Launching Writing Workshop Demonstration Lessons

workshop. Ideally, I wanted to end the workshop with five title options for each student.

Christine also picked up on the fact that there was a range of sophistication among maps. Some students had intricate maps and had generated many stories, while a few of the students had relatively blank maps. She wondered if all of her students would be able to generate stories from this strategy and wanted to know what you do when a student tells you the next day that he or she still has nothing to write about.

It turns out that Christine was right on with her thinking. This strategy of having students sketch out a setting map worked for most of the students, but not all of them. We decided to spend a few more days working with students digging up stories that they might want to write about (see Figure 2.7). In hopes of helping them generate story ideas, we ended up presenting the class with several different brainstorming strategies that we found in *How to Write Your Life Story* by Ralph Fletcher. After the setting map, we went on to explore special people in their lives and also significant possessions that might tell a story.

Modeling Anecdotal Notes During Demonstration Lessons

The observations I make of students during a lesson guide me in my instructional planning. I want to model for new teachers how formative assessment is incorporated into all that we do and that our plans are constantly changing based on the needs of our students.

During the lesson on mapping, I took quick student jottings on a sticky note. They were simple and were intended for just Christine and me. On this particular sticky note (see Figure 2.8), I was keeping track of students who had not yet generated any titles. I noted that Trez was motivated by a plus mark on his paper and that taking dictation was a strategy that was effective with him. I also noted that Katie was the last to get story ideas. She never drew any attention to herself, and I wanted to keep my eye on her since she was so quiet and could possibly slip through the cracks. The last student I wrote down was a student who had generated great ideas on his setting map (see Figure 2.9).

Figure 2.8
Student
Observation
Sticky Note

Jackson
Trez - dictated
        Needed support to get started
        Motivated by ④ on paper
        End of class asked, →"Can I share my map on the overhead."
Katie - Last to get story ideas
        Watch!
        Wrote same titles twice
+Nate - Strong, Rich Stories, Map
        "Love Manhunt. I want to write about that first."

Figure 2.9
Nate's Map and
Titles

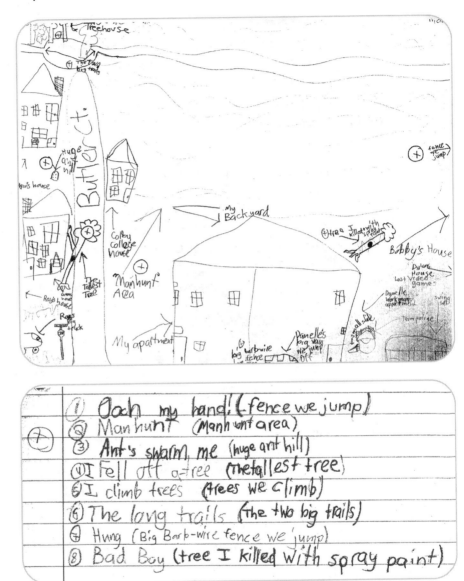

I wanted to keep an eye on him to make sure that I tapped his full potential as a writer.

At the end of the lesson, Christine and I immediately did a quick debrief so that she could hear my thoughts behind the student notes. This also gave her a chance to process her observations with me, and together we shared some quick thoughts about where we needed to go the next day.

Immediate debriefs help us focus on the kids instead of on teachers' self-consciousness about their role in the classroom. The power of this type of debrief isn't just that teachers get the feedback that they crave, but also that the presence of the kids jogs memories about specific interactions and learning, more so than we would get if we were debriefing much later.

Observing the Coach: Years Two and Three

I recently started a yoga class. I have never taken yoga, and I am not familiar with any of the poses. At the first class, I found myself completely dependent on the instructor. I think I spent more time watching from my mat than actually doing any of the poses. I needed her modeling so that I could get a better sense of what the poses should look like. I didn't have any background experiences that I could connect this new learning to and really needed to watch and learn.

Between sessions I needed to practice independently. The problem was that I couldn't remember my poses. I had a hard time making what some would call obvious connections. In the midst of trying to practice a pose, I asked my seven-year-old daughter if my downward dog pose looked right. She looked at me and said, "You know who does that pose all the time? Zoe." I was thinking, Zoe, our dog? when she said, "Mom, why do you think it is called downward dog?" And then it clicked for me—I finally had a connection and a visual for what the pose should look like. I wasn't ready to be independent quite yet!

As time went on and I became more confident and began to experiment and try out new yoga poses on my own, I was no longer so dependent on the instructor or my daughter for guidance. However, it was still comforting to know that whenever I was unsure of a move, all I had to do was ask the instructor for help and she would come over and move my limbs to help me achieve the desired position—at least to the extent my body would cooperate!

This example of gradual release is the same for demonstration lessons with teachers in their second and third year of teaching. As new teachers become more confident and more comfortable experimenting with new ideas in the classroom, they need me less and less. But that doesn't mean new teachers in their first few years of teaching can cut the cord completely.

In Jessica's second year of teaching, she wanted to put together an animal research project for her students where they would research an animal of choice through layering a variety of nonfiction books. We met a few times, and I listened as she created a skeleton structure for the project. I shared graphic organizers that students would use for taking notes and organizing their thinking, and together we gathered some animal books for students.

She began the unit on her own with her class. Within a few days, she was frustrated. She had started her students on note taking and had found that the students were not reading the texts but merely flipping through them. They were telling her that they were finished with the books and that they could not find any information. As a side note, Jess and I had actually purchased a variety of accessible animal texts specifically for this project. We handpicked the books because of their readability and the amount of information found within them. We had ensured that her room was filled with books rich with information on their chosen animals.

Jess came to me and asked if I would come in to her class during her literacy block and demonstrate how I might reintroduce the books to her kids. They had flown through the books and were telling her that they were ready to move on, and yet she didn't feel they were gathering the needed information. She feared that if she continued to move forward, their research would ultimately fall flat. It was her self-reflection that prompted her to evaluate the success of the animal unit and reach out for support. I worked my schedule so that I could get right into her room the next day.

During my demonstration visit, I let students know that we would be working with only one of their animal books for the day. Students had four or five core books that they were using to start their research, and I asked them to choose just one and to put the rest of the books, notes, and graphic organizers away. I wanted to slow the process and have students spend the reading period focused just on reading and talking about their animals. My purpose was to have them build more of a background knowledge base for their animal before starting the note-taking process.

Over the course of the forty-five minutes, I had students read independently for ten minutes at a time. At the end of a ten-minute block of time, I would ask students to jot on a sticky note one interesting fact they read that they thought a classmate might be interested in hearing. Students would then share their new learning for a few minutes in small groups. I asked if anyone wanted to share an interesting fact that they learned from a classmate. We then started the reading process again. We were able to get through about three reading cycles using this method.

In our debrief Jess noticed that the students were enthusiastic to share their new learning with classmates and were equally excited to share interesting facts with the class that they had had heard in the small-group talk time. We discussed the fact that the students might need more time to build their background knowledge on the animals prior to starting the note-taking process. After watching the lesson, Jessica decided to spend a few more days having her students read their books and talk about their new learning prior to any note taking. She was going to use the same strategy but have students pull out another core animal book. Through this demonstration, Jessica saw that sometimes you need to back up in order to move forward, that instruction doesn't always move in a straight line.

Drop-in visits like this one with Jess happen more with second- and third-year new teachers, who have a high comfort and skill level because of the many hours we have already put in together. This type of demonstration lesson—where the new teacher and I have less communication on a daily basis—is very different from one with a first-year teacher, but equally important, for it fosters experimentation as teachers continue to evolve and grow as educators.

Learning to Judge One's Effectiveness

I believe that our effectiveness as teachers is reflected through the learning of our students, not through showcase lessons. Having new teachers observe the coach provides them with a chance to see the internal self-monitoring process that teachers go through on a day-to-day basis as they reflect on student learning. It is my hope that, through observing other teachers and coaches, new teachers embrace self-reflection, observation, and experimentation and that they learn that good lessons build upon one another and that effective teachers constantly self-monitor, modify plans, and take risks to support student learning—whether or not they are being observed.

CHAPTER THREE

Administering and Analyzing Assessments

*Not everything that counts can be counted and not everything
that can be counted counts.*

ALBERT EINSTEIN

In the fall of my first year of teaching I had to administer the Analytical Reading Inventory (ARI) by Woods and Moe to all of my students. I was not familiar with this particular reading assessment. In fact, I don't recall having worked with any informal reading assessments during my undergraduate years.

The literacy specialist at the time graciously sat with me and gave me a quick overview of the ARI, an assessment that needs to be administered individually. Students read a passage orally to the teacher, who then asks a series of questions based on the text. Upon scoring the ARI, teachers get a glimpse of students' reading strategies and an approximate reading level for each student. I am sure the literacy specialist tried to explain to me all that I could learn about a student through the assessment, but all I heard and took in were the literal directions on how to administer it. I was caught up in my own sense of being overwhelmed with figuring out how to administer this assessment to individual students while the rest of the kids were in the room.

Somehow I managed. I say *somehow* since my classroom management strategies were lacking, to say the least.

After administering the reading assessments, I then had to meet with my building principal to go over my scores. I recall talking strictly levels and numbers. Some students were pushed up a reading grade level; others were lowered based on our discussion. I don't remember actually looking at student reading assessments during this meeting, just my class list and their reading levels. In no way did I view this assessment as a tool to analyze my students' oral reading behaviors or reading comprehension of the passage. Using assessments to inform instruction was not on my radar at the time. In my crash-course meeting with the literacy specialist, I had learned simply how to administer and score the assessment.

As a new teacher I was clueless in regard to the purpose of literacy assessment. All I knew was that it was just one more task I had to get done before I could check it off my to-do list.

The Disconnect Between Data and Students

I saw this same disconnect I had between assessment data and real students when I started working with new teachers. I remember asking them about their fall assessments at one of our meetings. I said, "So now that you have finished administering the assessments, what do you know about your students?" The group was silent. Some ruffled through their mound of student assessments, but most had not even brought them; instead, they stared blankly at their data sheet—a spreadsheet just filled with numbers, numbers that reflected reading levels, spelling levels, and writing-prompt scores.

It was an aha moment. I realized right then and there that what many of the teachers saw on that piece of paper was just what I had seen eighteen years ago—numbers, not their students. The reality was that it takes years to learn to read assessment data and know what it means for instruction and that you can confer with kids one on one only if your classroom routines and management are firmly in place—and all that is really tough for a new teacher. I think I was expecting too much too soon without offering any support.

I knew it was critical for new teachers to have some understanding of why we assess students. In my role, I wanted to better communicate the different purposes for fall and spring assessments, the intended audiences for that data, and the way to read it.

Why Do We Assess Students in the Fall?

Our purpose for administering fall literacy assessments to all students is for teachers to determine instructional needs and to set student goals (see Figure 3.1). These fall assessments are both diagnostic and formative: diagnostic since they let us know the level at which the student is working, and formative in the sense that they are assessments for learning (Chappuis and Chappuis 2007/2008). The results of our fall assessments are used to help the teacher make decisions on what to teach next. The primary audience for these results is the teacher, but they are also shared with parents at conference time, with the principal during literacy review meetings, and with me, since I maintain a database of all the literacy data. The purpose for the data at this time of year is to serve as a vehicle to allow us to keep our eye on all the students, watching out for any who may be slipping academically.

Audiences for Fall Data

- **Teachers.** Teachers use the fall data to inform their instruction and to make decisions on what to teach to students. Teachers set goals for students.
- **Parents.** Assessment results are shared with parents to inform them of their child's literacy development.

Figure 3.1

FALL LITERACY ASSESSMENTS, GRADES 3–5

- **Developmental Reading Assessment (Pearson Learning Company)**
  Students read from a selection of leveled texts. This assessment looks at reading engagement, oral reading fluency, and reading comprehension. An independent reading level is identified based on the total score achieved on the assessment rubric.

- **Elementary Spelling Inventory (Words Their Way)**
  Students are asked to spell a list of words and are then assessed on their word knowledge of specific spelling features. The assessment identifies their developmental stage of spelling.

- **Local Writing Prompt**
  Students are asked to respond to a prompt and produce a piece of on-demand writing. The prompt is narrative and reflects the genre expectations of the state. This is a locally designed assessment that reflects the scoring procedures of the MEA (Maine Educational Assessment).

- **Administrators.** Teachers review literacy data with principals during literacy meetings.
- **Literacy Specialists.** I maintain a literacy database with student data and keep an overall eye on it, making sure students are not falling through the cracks and working with teachers to identify those who would benefit from additional literacy support.

Why Do We Assess Students in the Spring?

The literacy assessments given in the fall are then readministered to our students in the spring. Summative in their purpose, spring assessments are often referred to as assessments *of* learning. They are used to measure student, school, and/or program success (Chappuis and Chappuis 2007/2008).

In the spring, data is reviewed at both the classroom level and the school level. Teachers review their own class data looking at growth of individual students and trends within their classrooms. And once all the student data is compiled and sorted, it is then reviewed and analyzed at the school/district level by grade-level teams.

It is at the team level that teachers work together and look for trends within the data and among different subgroups of students. Teachers review the data and make recommendations that would improve student learning and instructional practice.

Audiences for Spring Data

- **Teachers.** Teachers use spring data to examine individual student growth over the year and also look for trends within their own class.
- **Parents.** Assessment results are shared with parents to inform them of their child's growth in literacy.
- **District.** Literacy data is shared among all grade-level teachers, administrators, and the Board of Education. Data is reviewed and district goals are set based on results.
- **State.** The literacy data is sorted and analyzed by grade level and is used in the Title 1A report that is submitted to the state department of education.

The Power of Assessments

Donald Graves writes in *The Energy to Teach*, "Evaluation ought to be one of the greatest energy givers for the teacher in the classroom. The best teachers evaluate from the time the first child enters the classroom until she leaves" (2001, 82). Supporting new teachers and new staff through the local assessment process not only brings consistency to how assessments are administered and interpreted throughout the district, but, more importantly, communicates to new teachers the value of these assessments and how they can be used to get to know students and inform teacher instruction. I want the teachers I work with to learn the value of assessments and feel the "energy" that they can provide us.

Guiding and Modeling the Literacy Assessment Process

In both the fall and the spring, new teachers are given two release days out of their classrooms to administer, score, and analyze their student assessments. Substitutes are hired to cover the classrooms. The first day is used to administer the student assessments, and the second day is dedicated to working with new teachers in scoring and analyzing them. It is important to note that all teachers in our district are given one full release day to administer assessments to students in both fall and spring. During these release days, teachers set up throughout quiet parts of the school and pull students out of their classrooms one at a time or in small groups. The difference of support with new teachers is that they are given an additional release day to work with me to review their literacy assessments with the purpose of identifying student strengths and needs. The bottom line being, now that you have assessed your students, what can you learn about them through their assessments?

Supporting Christine Through Fall Assessments

To start the assessment process, I met with Christine to find out her familiarity and comfort levels with the assessments that we administer to students within our district. Together we looked through the fall literacy materials: the expectations (Figure 3.2), the literacy notebook, and the data recording sheet (Figure 3.3; also in appendix). Christine had administered the Developmental Reading Assessment during her undergraduate work but felt that the experience was quite limited and that she would welcome a refresher in it.

Together we plotted out a manageable schedule for administering the assessments (Figure 3.4). I encouraged Christine to administer as many of them as she could during reading and writing workshop because I wanted

Sample of Fall Literacy Expectations, Grade 4

Purpose

The purpose of administering fall literacy assessments is to determine instructional needs of students and to set student goals.

Sign up for a Literacy Release Day with the office for the week of September 22nd.

Reading

Administer Developmental Reading Assessment (DRA) to students. (See Literacy Notebook for procedures for administering DRA.)

Text Selection Fall: A New School Experience (Level 40)

Step 1: Student Reading Survey (A)

Step 2: One-on-One Student Reading Conference (B)

    ✓ If a child's reading rate is less than sixty words per minute, abandon the text and back down to a lower text level.

Step 3: Independent Student Work (C)

Step 4: Score and Record Assessment

    ✓ Analyze student written responses to select descriptors on the continuum, and determine student score and record on Teacher Observation Guide.

Record DRA Independent Reading Level on the Literacy Data Sheet (Example: Independent 3)

Writing

- Administer the writing prompt.
- Scoring will be done individually by teachers to inform instruction (copies of scoring rubrics in assessment folder).
- Fall anchor papers are in literacy notebooks.

Record Standard (D=Does Not Meet, PM=Partially Meets, M=Meets, E=Exceeds) on the Literacy Data Sheet

Spelling

- Administer the Elementary Spelling Inventory.
- Record the instructional spelling stage:
  - ✓ Early (E), Middle (M), Late (L)
  - ✓ E=Emergent, LN=Letter Name, WW=Within Word, SA=Syllables & Affixes, DR=Derivational Relations

Record Instructional Stage on the Literacy Data Sheet (Example: E–SA)

*Literacy Data Sheets due by October 10.

Figure 3.2

LITERACY DATA RECORDING SHEET

Teacher: _____   Grade: _____

| Last Name | First Name | Sp/Ed Speech | ESOL | New Entry | Reading | | Writing | | Spelling | | Research |
					Fall	Spring	Fall	Spring	Fall	Spring	Spring

Figure 3.3

ASSESSMENTS CALENDAR

Monday	Tuesday	Wednesday	Thursday	Friday
1 Labor Day No School	**2**	**3**	**4**	**5**
8 Administer Student Reading Survey DRA	**9**	**10**	**11**	**12**
15 Administer Writing Prompt	**16**	**17**	**18**	**19**
22 Administer Spelling Inventory	**23**	**24**	**25**	**26**
29 Release Day Coverage in Classroom *Start DRAs Jen models administering the oral reading fluency and comprehension component of the DRA working 1:1 with Christine	**30**			Release Day Coverage in Classroom Score Assessments with Christine in Literacy Room

Figure 3.4

her to see how meaningful assessments can be a part of the day rather than an "extra" that she needed to fit in.

Christine planned on having her fourth-grade students complete the fall writing prompt during her writing workshop time. The reading survey for the Developmental Reading Assessment (DRA) and the Elementary Spelling Inventory were to be administered during reading workshop.

After we plotted out the assessment schedule, I continued my support as I worked with Christine in helping her implement her fall assessments for the first time. Prior to her first literacy release day, Christine administered the reading survey from the DRA to her whole class, dictated the spelling words for the Elementary Spelling Inventory, and had her students complete the district's fall writing prompt.

During her first literacy release day, we worked on administering the DRA to her students. Since she was not familiar with the assessment, I modeled administering the oral reading fluency and comprehension components of the DRA for her with several students. After each one, we talked about what we saw and recorded our observations. For example, one of the first students read at 125 words a minute. Typically that would place him in the independent range for reading rate. Although this student read at what we would call an adequate rate, his phrasing was completely inappropriate. We questioned if he was reading for any meaning. He seemed to be highly motivated by the stopwatch. Christine and I talked about watching his comprehension on the rest of the assessment and also focusing in on him in the classroom to make sure that as a reader he wasn't putting too much emphasis on his reading rate for the sacrifice of his comprehension.

Gradual Release

During the course of the day, I transitioned from giving the DRA as Christine watched and listened to letting Christine administer the assessment as I watched and listened, and, eventually, to moving away from the table as Christine administered the DRA independently. I stayed in the room working just so that I could be available in case she encountered any questions.

Christine was not afraid to ask questions. One of her students read with 99 percent word accuracy but had a reading rate of fifty-eight words per minute. At this rate, the assessment indicated that the child needed to drop to a lower level. In this case, Christine wanted me to affirm that she should administer a lower-level text to the student.

In another case, Christine noticed that one of her students wrote very little on the independent writing section of the level 40 DRA (fourth-grade text). The student was supposed to complete this section independently. Christine showed me that the child wrote very little in response to the text questions. By being there, I was able to reinforce that we use these assessments to learn about the students. In this situation I asked her to bring the student back and take dictation for the questions and try to find out what the child knew from the story. Maybe this was a writing issue? Maybe the student struggled to communicate his thinking through writing? Maybe the student didn't understand the text? The key is that we don't settle for a blank summary and question section. It is not all about the score, but rather about trying to unearth what our students can do and taking note of the strategies that we use as teachers that support their success.

Pulling It All Together: Using Fall Assessments to Know Your Students

Assessments are tools—tools that help us learn more about our students as learners, and this is the purpose of administering fall assessments. Ultimately, these assessment tools should inform our instruction.

New teachers are given a second release day so that they can take the time to review their scores and analyze their student assessments. This is the critical aspect of support that was missing when I first worked with new teachers on assessments. It is the day we spend looking at and learning about students through their fall literacy assessments. When I first did this, I worked with all the new teachers on the same release day. I found it was too many people to work with at once to be effective. I couldn't get around and spend enough time with each teacher and provide the individualized attention that was needed for this type of analysis. I now usually work with just one or two teachers at the most on this second release day.

To help guide them in their reflection on student assessments, I adapted an organizer from Joanne Hindley that was presented in her book *In the Company of Children* (1996). (See Figure 3.5; also in appendix.) I wanted something that was user-friendly and that would reflect a quick snapshot of the child. It was designed for teachers to look at the assessment and record their overall sense of the child's strengths and needs. I know there is not a lot of room to write. The form was not designed to record every detail learned from the assessment but rather to record the overall message that can be extracted from it. The purpose is to gather student information (beyond numbers and levels) so that we can use the information to inform instruction. I ask new teachers to reflect on the following questions:

- What does the student know? (+)
- What does the student need to know? (–)
- How can we go about meeting their needs? (*)

What does this look like in action? Christine used these questions to guide her as she looked at each student individually through their assessments.

USING ASSESSMENTS TO INFORM INSTRUCTION

Student	Developmental Reading Assessment (DRA)	Writing Prompt and Writing Sample	Elementary Spelling Inventory

Figure 3.5

Looking Through Christine's Assessments

Christine and I spent her second release day together looking through all of her student assessments. To launch this process, I asked Christine to select one of her students and to pull all of his or her fall assessments and any related anecdotal notes that she had made so that we could look at the whole child. She decided to start with a student named Jacob. Jacob was an interesting kid and a definite surprise. He was highly verbal in the classroom and was always engaged during class discussions. When we went through his fall assessments, Christine and I were surprised to find that he was working below grade-level expectations in both reading and writing. He was a child that we both thought was performing at a higher level. My observations and work in Christine's classroom led me to think he was at least working at grade level. But he was also a student who was not always engaged during times of independent work. Jacob was definitely a student we would continue to watch and try to figure out.

Jacob's Fall Assessments
- Developmental Reading Assessment—Instructional Level 34
- Writing Prompt—Did Not Meet Grade-Level Expectations
- Spelling—Late Syllable Affix

Christine's Classroom Observations of Jacob
- Strong verbal skills
- Not always engaged during independent work, a lot of time spent getting up for materials

Student	Developmental Reading Assessment (DRA)	Writing Prompt and Writing Sample	Elementary Spelling Inventory
Jacob	+Decodes −Needs to use evidence from the text to support thinking *Continue to find strategies that will allow him to communicate this thinking and what he knows	+Strong title +Generates topic −Writing lacks development *Continue to find strategies that will engage him in writing	+Late Syllable Affix +Demonstrates application in personal writing *Continue word study

Using Assessments to Inform Instruction

- What Does the Student Know (+)?
- What Does the Student Need to Know (-)?
- How Can We Go About Meeting Their Needs (*)?

Student	Developmental Reading Assessment (DRA)	Writing Prompt &Writing Sample	Elementary Spelling Inventory
Jacob	+ decoding – Engagement * Evidence from text	+ Titles, Generates Topics – Engaged * Develop Writing	+ Application + Solid Word Study Foundation * Continue Word Study
Shayna	+ Strong fluency – Comprehension	+ Begins on topic – Details * Develop details	+ diagram, blends – Long Vowel patterns * Short Vowels l+v
Catherine	+ Comprehension – rate * phrasing, rate	+ word choice – sentence variety * mentor texts modeling	+ where she needs to be (SA) * Continue Word Study Prefix Suffix
Emily	+ Appropriate book choices + engaged * Work on Comprehension	+ Generates Text * Continue topic development	+ high frequency words * Continue Word Study
Ethan	+ Reading Interpreting – Summarizing	+ Topic development – word choice sentence variety	+ where he needs to be syllable affix * Continue Word Study
Owen	+ self correcting for meaning * Increase Rate, stamina	+ Begin, mid, end – details * Support development	+ where he needs to be (SA) * Continue Word Study
Jonathan	+ Self Monitors + self corrects 52 wpm * (–) Increase Rate	+ Communicate thinking verbally * Work on Preparing through writing	+ short vowel – long vowel pattern * Word Study

Figure 3.6
Christine's Using Assessments to Inform Instruction

After reviewing the first few students with her, Christine reviewed the rest on her own (see Figure 3.6). She would often share her thinking with me, and at times I would review the student assessments confirming what she saw in the child or maybe nudge her to look at them again. I tried to hold back and not share too much of my thinking (which is hard for me), since it is the new teacher who needs to learn how to see the student through the assessments. Only after Christine went through all of the assessments did she record her student literacy score on the data sheet (see Figure 3.7). Her process of sorting through fall data was a great example of how she looked at kids first and numbers last.

Supporting Veteran Teachers New to the School

Ray, a teacher new to our school but not new to teaching, also participated in the two release days for administering and analyzing fall assessments. He had ten years of teaching experience but still welcomed the time to

Christine's Literacy Report

Teacher: Christine   **Grade: 4**

Last Name	First Name	Sp/Ed Speech	ESOL	New Entry	Reading		Writing		Spelling		Research
					Fall	Spring	Fall	Spring	Fall	Spring	Spring
	Jacob				2		DNM		L-SA		
	Shayna				2		DNM		M-VVV		
	Catherine				3		PM		M-SA		
	Emily				2		DNM		L-VVV		
	Ethan				3		PM		L-SA		
	Owen				2		DNM		L-SA		
	Jonathan				3		DNM		L-LN		
	Mary				3		PM		L-VVV		
	Alex				4		PM		L-SA		
	Toby				2		PM		M-VVV		
	Daniel				3		M		M-SA		
	Hannah				4		PM		L-SA		
	Nathan				3		PM		L-SA		
	Nathan				3		PM		L-SA		
	Tyler				3		M		L-DR		
	Jake				3		PM		M-DR		
	Kellie				3		DNM		M-DR		
	Troy				3		PM		L-SA		
	Katie				3		DNM		E-SA		
	Sarah				3		DNM		L-SA		

Figure 3.7

become familiar with our district's literacy expectations. And although he had extensive experience in student reading and writing behaviors and understood how to use assessments to inform instruction, he wasn't familiar with our specific literacy assessments. Ray shared that the release days were a gift. He went on to explain to me that as a veteran teacher it had been hard getting e-mails with lots of educational acronyms that he hadn't quite internalized yet, from people with names that he couldn't quite put faces to. He was hesitant to ask the questions that he knew he needed to ask since he felt like he should already know all of it. Transitioning to a new school, new state, and new grade level has its own new unexpected learning curve as one becomes familiar with the nuts and bolts of the assessment system.

Moving Beyond Mountains of Data

It seems that over the past few years we have been buried in mountains of data. We have looked at numbers and subgroups every which way. And yet, through all the numbers, it's hard to see individual kids.

Supporting new teachers through the assessment process and helping them analyze the actual assessments benefits both the teachers and the students. New teachers come away from the process of reviewing and analyzing with a renewed sense of confidence. They not only internalize the relevant purpose for administering assessments, but they also walk away with a better sense of their students' strengths and needs as learners.

New teachers entering our system must learn how to look beyond the mounds of assessment papers and numbers and feel the energy that Donald Graves said that evaluations ought to give off. We need to keep students at the heart of our conversations and use assessments to inform and guide our instruction.

CHAPTER FOUR

In-Class Support: Establishing Structures

To coach means to convey a valued colleague from where he or she is to where he or she wants to be.

ARTHUR COSTA AND ROBERT J. GARMSTON, 1994

My seven-year-old daughter takes gymnastics lessons. I have watched in amazement over the last year at how her coach breaks down instruction. Before ever beginning a recognizable cartwheel, he works with students on hand placement on mats. Backward rolls are started on an inclined mat, and students work on formation and feeling the weight on their arms. After the coach's initial demonstration, student volunteers provide continued modeling as needed visual supports, and his students spend their class practicing and working through moves on various equipment.

Over time I have watched the coach slowly remove scaffolds, such as the tape on the floor for cartwheels or the inclined mats for backward rolls. And his students are now doing those moves without missing any of the accommodations that had been in place for them over the last year. As the instructional coach, he continues to observe, support, and demonstrate as needed and is available to his students, with the ultimate goal of moving them forward to be independent gymnasts who bring their own individual zest to the mat.

As I watched Samantha at gymnastics, I couldn't help but think of my first year of teaching. As a new educator, I landed the job and was set free with twenty-three students. Oh, how I could have benefited from an instructional coach, someone who could have supported me as I transitioned from the world of textbooks and university work to the reality of classroom teaching.

Gradual Release Model Over Three Years

Just like the gymnastics coach, I demonstrate, observe, and support, and I am available to the new teachers so that they feel safe trying out new instructional strategies while I guide them toward independence. As a coach, I not only want to be there to support instruction but I also want to foster a sense of individuality. One of my goals in working with new teachers is to support them in a way that nurtures them to become the teacher they want to be.

I follow a gradual release model of support with new teachers (Pearson and Gallagher 1983). In this model the staff developer provides explicit instruction. Gradually, through guided and independent practice, the responsibility and application of new learning shifts from the staff developer to the teacher. Being the one who teaches and being observed by the new teacher is the modeling stage of gradual release.

"Staff development research reports to us loud and clear that it is the follow-up (assessing and assisting), the checking back with individuals as they are trying to use new ideas in their work setting, that makes or breaks the success of implementation" (Horde and Sommers 2008, 135). Knowing that the most effective support for teachers is that which is ongoing and embedded within the classroom setting, I support new teachers within their classrooms over the course of several years.

What does this support look like over time (see Figure 4.1)? The first year I tend to work in a new teacher's classroom three times a week for at least forty-five minutes; the following year I work in the classroom once a week, but still collaborate with plans; and the third year I drop in and work in the room as needed. In the third year I am working to wean myself out of the room, and although I touch base weekly with the teacher for planning purposes, when I go into the classroom, I follow his or her lead. I am there to support teachers' thinking, to talk through strategies for students who are puzzling them, and to help them work through any other roadblocks that they may encounter. During these years of support, I am working with teachers to be critical, self-reflective practitioners.

OVERVIEW OF THREE YEARS OF IN-CLASS SUPPORT FOR JESSICA

Sample Schedule of a Week in Year One

Monday	Tuesday	Wednesday	Thursday	Friday
9:30–10:15 Writing Workshop	9:30–10:15 Writing Workshop	9:30–10:15 Writing Workshop	9:30–10:15 Writing Workshop	9:30–10:15 Writing Workshop
In-class support	In-class support	In-class support	Jessica Independent	Jessica Independent
Jessica's room	Jessica's room	Jessica's room		
			Meet with Jessica during prep period for planning	

Sample Schedule of a Week in Year Two

Monday	Tuesday	Wednesday	Thursday	Friday
9:30–10:15 Writing Workshop	9:30–10:15 Writing Workshop	9:30–10:15 Writing Workshop	9:30–10:15 Writing Workshop	9:30–10:15 Writing Workshop
Jessica Independent	Jessica Independent	Jessica Independent	In-class support	Jessica Independent
			Jessica's room	
			Meet with Jessica during prep period for planning	

Sample Schedule of a Week in Year Three

Monday	Tuesday	Wednesday	Thursday	Friday
9:30–10:15 Writing Workshop	9:30–10:15 Writing Workshop	9:30–10:15 Writing Workshop	9:30–10:15 Writing Workshop	9:30–10:15 Writing Workshop
Jessica Independent	Jessica Independent	Jessica Independent	Jessica Independent	In-class support
				Jessica's room— *as requested*; follow Jessica's lead

Meet or e-mail in response to Jessica's needs.

Figure 4.1

In order to provide new teachers with this level of support, I needed to reevaluate and prioritize how and where I spent my time. The sacrifice that I needed to make was reducing my work with veteran teachers. There just wasn't enough time to work with everyone who wanted coaching support. Now, in setting my own calendar, the first blocks of time go to working with new teachers. I do try to set aside time to work with one veteran teacher a year on an inquiry project. My schedule will continue to change each year as the number of new teachers waxes and wanes.

When talked about and written down on calendars, it looks and sounds like such a clean, linear process, with a miraculous transfer of learning between coach and new teacher. However, my reality is that this process is anything but linear. And most of the time it is downright murky. The only constant is my actual schedule for in-class support—support that is varied and individualized, depending on the needs and desires of the teachers I work with.

The First Year of Support

I tend to hold off from providing support in classrooms until at least the third week of school. I think it is important for new teachers to have time in their classrooms alone to get to know their students and establish classroom routines and procedures before I start coming into the room. They must have some time to figure out what they need and how I can best support them.

Just because I am not in their rooms doesn't mean we are not meeting and touching base on an almost daily basis. Those first few weeks for new teachers are all about setting the stage for the year. Right at the start of school I usually find myself helping new teachers think about how they want to launch reading workshop—do they want to do an author study or maybe a whole-class book? I spend time suggesting resources but have them make the decisions about how they want to start their year. I support them in administering their fall literacy assessments (see Chapter 3). I am also often stopping in before and after school, making sure that they have all the materials and tools that they need for students (notebooks, folders, sticky notes, highlighters, organizational crates). These informal meetings provide an opportunity for new teachers to raise any compelling issues that concern them.

As I transition into a new teacher's classroom, I try to work within the learning environment that the teacher has established; this includes reinforcing the behavior-management system the teacher already has in place, delivering lessons using the existing room arrangement, and utilizing the equipment in the room.

Management First!

As a first-year teacher, I naively thought that I was well equipped in the area of classroom management. I had handled a few challenging students in my student-teaching experience and was not worried about classroom management. I had read all about William Glasser's Reality Therapy (1990) and believed that if all students took responsibility for their learning and had logical consequences for behaviors, we would have a well-oiled classroom filled with students who respected their learning environment and had a sense of belonging and who longed for learning. I remember even saying in my initial classroom interviews that classroom management was one of my strengths! Well, my overconfidence in behavior management should have been a red flag to someone right there. Glasser's Reality Therapy failed me! Even implementing a bathroom pass system seemed to be near impossible for me. My management was awful. My students ran the class. I can still see one of my students, Josh, standing up on the radiator, swatting a bee with a rolled-up piece of paper, trying to "save us" as the class shouted on about the bee in our room. I had no control. It was loud, it was messy, and all my energy went into trying to manage students.

The reality is that you can't move into instructional issues if students are not engaged as a result of behaviors interfering with learning. So even though I am a literacy coach, I spend a great deal of time that first year working with new teachers talking through room arrangement and behavior-management plans. I learned early on that as a new teacher you needed a plethora of management strategies—that one system would not work for all students. Knowing the importance of being armed with a variety of strategies, I want new teachers to be exposed to multiple possibilities for management to suit their personalities. In addition to my support as they implement management in their classrooms, new teachers have ongoing opportunities to observe the classroom management strategies of other teachers through peer observations (see Chapter 6).

Year One: Christine

Christine decided that she wanted my support in establishing writing workshop within her classroom. I encourage teachers to select writing workshop for coaching since it's such a foundation for lots of other things. The plan was that I would work with her in her room for forty-five minutes three times a week and help her launch writing workshop. But, just as I had learned my first year of teaching, Christine soon realized that her immediate challenge was not instruction, but room arrangement and behavior management.

Room Arrangement

Behavior management and room arrangement tend to go hand in hand. I find that the room arrangement of a new teacher often reflects the challenges that they face with classroom management.

One of the first things that I noticed when I started working in Christine's room was that her desks were arranged in rows. I personally love student desks arranged in groups and like to be able to move freely around the room and easily reach students. I tend to gravitate toward learning environments where students are physically grouped together and have opportunities for ongoing conversations during writing workshop. But, with that said, I am respectful of whatever room arrangement a teacher has implemented. I also understand the physical restraints of working in an old building with small classrooms and twenty-five growing bodies. In buildings like ours, it is sometimes hard to create that Debbie Miller learning environment that you dream of creating! I usually hold back from sharing how I would set up the room.

I gained insight into Christine's row arrangement the first day that I spent in her classroom. Her students were talkers. I don't mean talkers in a good way. They talked constantly—talking to each other, shouting out to Christine, and just plain yelling out for attention. I felt like I was at a basketball game, trying to follow the ball around the court. Except in this case I was trying to figure out all this talking. I had not seen anything quite like it in a while.

Debbie Miller points out that "classroom environments are most effective when they are literate and purposeful, organized and accessible, and, most of all, authentic" (2008, 23). That may be true, but one of the things I notice is that many new teachers start off the year with a sense of purpose in their room arrangement, such as having their desks in groups to foster collaboration, but quickly abandon their idea and put the desks in rows as a coping strategy for behavior management. And as in Christine's case, even though her desks were in rows, it didn't solve the issues surrounding behavior management.

Management isn't just about relationships with kids—it's about arrangements that inspire and calm them, helping them produce their best work. And as a coach, I have learned you have to be gentle in getting teachers to think about and change room arrangements. I too want new teachers to be purposeful in the design of their classroom environment but have learned that it takes time and much tweaking before they find the arrangement that works for them. Implementing effective room arrangement can be a process.

After a few weeks of school, I asked Christine to reflect on her room arrangement. I asked if the layout of her room was working out as she had hoped and, even more specifically, if the arrangement reflected her beliefs about student learning. Christine shared that her students talked out all the time and she didn't know what to do. She would love to have her students in groups but didn't think they—or she—could handle it. After spending time in her room and observing the talk pattern, I understood her issue. We discussed the placement of a few of her key students, including Trez. She had placed Trez in the front row so that he would pay attention, but she noticed that it wasn't working because he wouldn't stop turning around. He spent the whole class turned toward the back of the room interrupting classmates. I shared my wondering of what would happen if he was placed in the back of the room so he could watch everyone. The thinking was that if he turned around in the back row, he would be facing all of the coats and backpacks. The next day when I went in, Christine had moved Trez. She shared that turning around was no longer an issue for him. He now sat facing forward, able to see all of his peers in action.

Christine kept the rows but continued focusing in on individual student needs and moving students around to achieve different combinations. She did want a learning environment where students worked together in groups but wasn't quite ready to put them into groups yet.

Time went on. After several classroom observations Christine was inspired to rearrange her room again. She spent hours after school staying well into the evening with a colleague making the transformation. When I went into her room on the next day, she was proud to show me the changes. She had created a whole new classroom library, class meeting area, and desk setup—instead of all rows, only a few of the desks were left in rows; the rest were in groups.

Well, the story of room arrangement doesn't end there. The arrangement didn't exactly solve all of the talking issues that were directly interfering with instruction. As the weeks went on and Christine continued to work on classroom management, I slowly watched as the groups disappeared and the rows returned.

Did Christine's desk arrangement reflect her beliefs about teaching? No. But, for the time being, the arrangement helped her with behavior management. The students had responded to the arrangement. My prediction is that Christine will not have her students in rows next year. But for now, this is the least of her obstacles.

I see room arrangement as a process that evolves as new teachers begin "living" in their classrooms with students. It is important not to judge the effectiveness of new teachers based on their classroom arrangement—room design is all part of the learning process. I find that asking clarifying questions is an effective strategy to get them to reflect on their room arrangement.

Questions That Prompt Reflection on Room Arrangement
- Are you feeling comfortable with your room arrangement?
- Do you feel that the room arrangement lends itself to group work and collaboration?
- Is the setup of the classroom working for the students?
- Are you and the students able to get around the room and work freely?
- What are you thinking about the placement of materials for students? Are they accessible? Are you having any issues in this area?
- How is your class meeting area working? Is there enough room for all the bodies? Where else might you make space for a meeting area?

Behavior Management

In terms of behavior management I always try to follow the teacher's plan. But sometimes that plan doesn't work and we need to tweak it. Sometimes I don't hold the same philosophical beliefs regarding behavior-management systems. I have to be careful what I say though, because many times new teachers are getting ideas from other teachers within the school. So I try to remember and practice the quote I came across a few years ago by Dorothy Neville (ThinkExist.com): "The real art of conversation is not only to say the right thing at the right place but to leave unsaid the wrong thing at the tempting moment."

Christine was a reflective teacher from the start. All I did was ask one day if she thought her behavior-management plan of writing the name on the board for negative behavior was working. She opened up and shared her struggles and sought out suggestions and ideas from me and from other colleagues.

One of the things that Christine and I talked about was how to validate students who were working. How could we turn the behaviors in the classroom around from negative to positive? She shared that she felt that she was always focusing on those students who were interrupting the lesson.

One of the ideas that Christine implemented was a point system for students on task and engaged in their learning. She had gotten this idea from another teacher. As she caught students working, she gave them a check on a slip of paper taped to their desk. Point systems are an example of a time when I had to keep some of my personal feelings to myself. Christine and I talked about what to do with the points. Keeping true to my background with Glasser, and believing that the motivation to learn should be intrinsic, I cautioned Christine about giving students external rewards for good behavior. We brainstormed a list of rewards that were not material items and choices that did not cost money. The goal was to give students rewards that provided them with choices and control over their time and learning.

Christine then developed a menu of choices students could pick from to turn in their points.

Point Menu

All Choices 10 Points

- Fifteen minutes of free choice time
- Homework pass
- Lunch with the teacher
- Ticket for class movie and popcorn
- Treasure box
- Fifteen minutes of free computer time
- Choice of seat in writing workshop

Christine followed through on this idea and got the system up and running by the end of November. Many students were newly motivated, if not to learn, to earn points.

One day as I finished conferencing with Jake, one of her students, I commented to him that his piece was an example of strong writing and that I liked his word choice (it just so happened that Jake was one of the more challenging students for us to motivate). Jake looked at me, moved his paper, showing me his blank point sheet, and said, "My teacher usually gives me a check when I have done some quality work." Evidence that Jake was externally motivated by the new point system! I still held back about my feelings toward it.

If I want teachers to become independent and judge their own effectiveness, then I need to stand back and not always show them how I would do things. It would only reinforce a need to be affirmed with every decision and change that they make. But what I do is continue to model the inquiry process of identifying needs and modeling how we can uncover natural motivators.

Although the kids bought into the point system, I feared it might have been squelching internal motivation and discipline. Regardless, not all of our behavior-management issues were solved.

Before we knew it December was on our doorstep. I wanted to continue to model the inquiry process and look for a natural motivator that would be intrinsically motivating for students. My hope was to communicate to Christine that there are internal strategies that can be effective. Christine and I worked to identify what we saw as the biggest challenge. She felt that the number of students talking out about irrelevant topics was at the top of the list, since it was directly related to lack of student productivity. We knew we needed to get more of these children talking about writing. Too many of them were getting by doing a minimal amount of work throughout the day.

We decided to try using computers as a natural motivator. Our next strategy was to get students on the computers daily for writing workshop, and we were able to implement this by using the various resources within the school, bargaining computer time with other teachers and signing up for the computer lab or the mobile laptop cart four days out of the week. We arranged our writing workshop schedule and decided to have mini-lessons on Tuesday since that was the one day students did not have access to computers. The ability to use the computers for composition and the daily built-in share time within the writing workshop turned the writing class around faster than any point system. In fact, the point system was never reinforced in the computer lab, and students never asked about earning points while composing on the computers even though the system was still in place within the classroom. We saw immediate results in increased productivity of high-quality writing.

Again, Christine and I reflected on the behavior needs of the classroom. She shared that several of her students were subtly picking on another student, Kate, by doing things like not wanting to sit next to her or to compliment her writing. Christine and I started to really watch the kids and figure out which student was leading the way. It took only a few days to see it was a girl named Jackie who was the ringleader. She wasn't even the one doing the bullying, but the others would glance up to her for approval. The other issue was that in looking at Jackie's learning, we realized that she was slipping and not progressing. Christine had already shared her academic concerns with Jackie's parents at the fall parent/teacher conferences. I shared my student concerns with the principal and wondered what would happen if we moved Jackie into another classroom with a veteran teacher. The idea would be to better meet Jackie's learning needs and hopefully change the social dynamics within Christine's room to benefit the learning of the students. The principal supported the idea not because she was trying to ease the behaviors in Christine's room but because she was looking out for the learning of Jackie, just as she would for any other student. Jackie's parents agreed to the move, since they too were concerned about her learning.

The girl adjusted beautifully to her new teacher and classmates. The best news of all was that once Jackie moved into a new classroom, the other four students, all followers who were doing the harassing, started focusing on their own learning and stopped picking on Kate. I can't help but smugly think of a line from Jack Gantos's short story "The Follower": "And when you put two followers together nothing really bad happens" (2005, 82).

It wasn't until January that we were really on track and ready to dig deep into instruction. It was at that point that my role transitioned from supporting behavior management to coaching instruction.

I did end up supporting Christine in writing workshop throughout her first year of teaching, but we really did spend the first four months of school focusing in on and talking about room arrangement and behavior-management strategies. My goal for Christine during my second and third years of support will be that she independently implement and sustain writing workshop.

The Second and Third Years of Support

The second and third years of teaching are an opportunity for new teachers to define themselves as educators. I see these years as an opportunity for new teachers to refine instructional practice and put together the pieces of the curriculum.

The framework of layered support that I use for teachers in year one is the same for those in years two and three except for the amount of in-class support. I move from working in new-teachers' classrooms three days a week to only one day a week and start to move more and more into the background. The teachers take the lead and ownership of planning, but I remain a sounding board as their mentor for short- and long-range curriculum planning. Although I continue to provide in-class support, I am no longer the one leading the lesson. We both take anecdotal notes on stu-

Figure 4.2
Sample
Anecdotal
Notes and
Debrief

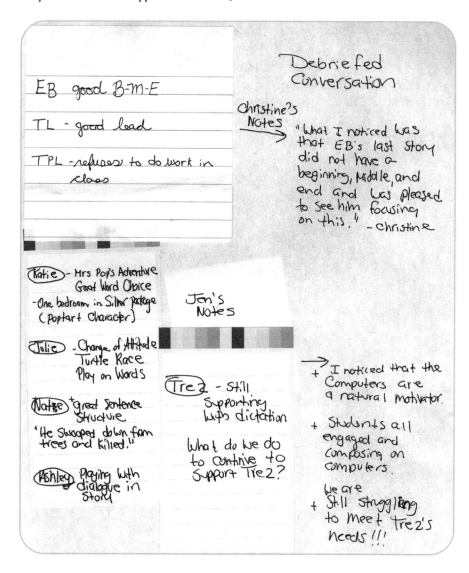

dents, and we still debrief at the end of lessons (see Figure 4.2). I continue to meet weekly as needed during a planning period to touch base and to work through obstacles that they may face.

Year Two: Page

Page is a second-year teacher. I go into her room once a week, and, while there, I will follow her lead. I still demonstrate lessons once in a while, but when I do, it is because Page has asked me to model a strategy or lesson that she wants to clarify for herself. Modeling gives her the opportunity to see an idea in action.

One of the issues that came up in meeting with Page at the beginning of her second year was that she was having trouble remembering what I did in her room for particular lessons the previous year. This is typical because a first-year teacher is so consumed with keeping her head above water that she doesn't take in all the instructional details. She was using the binders and our plans, but she couldn't recall the details. I reinforced the importance of making her writing workshop lessons her own and that the resources that I had pulled together for her in binders over the last year were just that, resources, and that she could use them to build off of.

Page also needed to find her own mentor texts, the ones that she loved and wanted to share with students. I had used the book *Grandpa Never Lies* by Ralph Fletcher in her room the previous year to get students thinking about special people in their lives. I pushed Page to find another book, one that she enjoyed and that could serve the same purpose. She came up with *Saturdays and Teacakes* by Lester Laminack. Page also used this second year to start generating some of her own stories and writing to share with students. She knew that I had used my personal writing in mini-lessons, and she wanted to be able to share some of her own.

Page took control in larger ways over weeks and months as she began to refine her own vision for her writing workshop. For example, she modified and improved a multigenre unit that we had done her first year by adding in another genre and having her students create a comic strip. Page also looked at her whole year of writing workshop and moved around genre studies to different months and added in more opportunities for her students to have choice writing.

Year Three: Jessica

Jessica no longer needs my support but still reaches out to me when she is working through a new idea. Jess keeps in touch through e-mail, and we have a working e-mail relationship. I will also go into her room on an as-needed basis.

In the e-mails that I receive from Jess, she often shares her new ideas and thinking. I listen through her typed words as she reflects and works through her own thinking. Jess is always reaching out and exploring new ways to stretch her students. Here are a few of our e-mail topics.

- **Launching Word Study**

  Jess was out on maternity leave at the beginning of the year and was worried about getting word study launched in her classroom. Over several e-mails we decided to pilot Words Their Way word-study notebooks with her class. It was an opportunity to pilot the notebooks and at the same time provide more structure to her word study, structure that might be more manageable for a substitute. I supported her by purchasing the notebooks for her students and working with the substitute to launch word study within Jess's classroom.

- **Class Blog**

  Jess was in her second year of refining an exploration of poetry with her students. She felt that they were writing but were not as into writing poetry as her class last year had been. We talked about ways that students could get authentic feedback and have a wider audience for their writing. Jess ended up creating a class blog so that students could post their poems and other students, parents, and community members could read them and comment. Jess also hooked up with The Farnum Writing Center at Colby College. Colby students provided ongoing comments to her class throughout the year. You can visit Jessica's blog, The Amazing Authors of Room 310, at http://mrssoucysclass.blogspot.com/.

- **Finding a Writing Idea Before Holiday Break**

  A few weeks before holiday break Jess was rethinking where she wanted to go with writing workshop. She had planned to move into research with her students but felt that they needed a break between genre studies. We went back and forth and talked about where students have opportunities to have control over and choice of their genre of writing during the year. Jess decided to give students a three-week block of choice writing between the genre studies. I was able to share a student planning sheet/assessment rubric with her that she was able to tweak for class.

- **Enriching Two Student Writers**

  Jess e-mailed that she had two brilliant writers, students who she truly felt would be published someday. She had shared with them that I had written a book. They were interested and wanted to know if I would meet with them to talk about my writing process and the publishing process.

Another example of specific support during Jess's third year of teaching was when she wanted feedback on a rubric that she was creating for a writing project (see Figure 4.3). She shared the rubric with me through

NONFICTION ANIMAL REPORT

Name: _____

	Meets	Partially Meets	Does Not Meet	I Noticed
Report begins with an introductory paragraph.				
One paragraph describes the animal's physical characteristics.				
One paragraph describes the animal's habitat.				
One paragraph tells about the animal's diet.				
One paragraph gives details about the animal's family life.				
Report ends with conclusion, and may tell about the future for this animal.				
Uses proper conventions (spelling, grammar, capitalization, punctuation, etc.).				

Figure 4.3
Jessica's Animal
Report Rubric

e-mail one night. I didn't propose that she change it. Instead I asked clarifying questions, such as, What is it that you want the students to be able to demonstrate through the research project? Jess shared that she wanted them to be able to read informational text, determine important information, and communicate their new thinking. Together, we generated note-taking headings (physical characteristics, habitat, diet, and family life) that would guide students in their research process. These headings were then worked into her final rubric to assess student learning. Jessica revised her initial rubric as she clarified her own expectations for the assigned project. This rubric was completed through our correspondence back and forth through e-mail that night as Jess worked through her thinking.

Changes in Support Over Time

Just as my daughter did in gymnastics, the new teachers that I work with have needed less explicit support over time. I find that I am still providing teachers in their third and fourth year of teaching with support—it just looks different than it did during that crucial first year. I am no longer in many of their classrooms on a weekly basis, nor do we have set meeting dates. As a literacy leader, I try to be there when they need me, but also give them space to grow as individuals. We want our students to develop self-extending systems so that they can independently self-monitor and identify problems in their learning. I wish for the same for the teachers I work with. I want them to be able to identify and seek support on their own before they are frustrated or struggling.

I still keep in contact with "new teachers" beyond years three and four when I am no longer consistently in their classrooms. What I notice about this phase of coaching is that as the teachers become more experienced and confident, they are not afraid to initiate contact and ask for support.

Lucy, in her fifth year of teaching, asked to meet for curriculum planning. She feared that her pacing was too slow to get through the grade-level curriculum and wanted help in plotting out her long-range plans for the spring. We met during one of her prep periods and looked at where her students were in literacy, reviewed curricular expectations, and tweaked her original plan. Since we have an established relationship and history together, it was easy to jump right in and focus on her immediate needs.

My daughter, Samantha, the budding gymnast, no longer needs the support of an incline for the backward roll. Teachers I've worked with for three or four years no longer need the formal support of me working with them in their classrooms. However, I am still there to help, and they are comfortable coming to me for resources or when issues emerge in their teaching, and they continue to have access to all the other professional development opportunities that we offer all teachers within our district.

CHAPTER FIVE

Meeting as a Group

We learn more in communities where learners and teachers foster
mutual respect; learn to know, value, and care for one another;
and feel comfortable enough to take risks.

SUSI LONG AND OTHERS, 2006

This past fall my son, Ben, ran cross-country. As I walked in the door after work, Ben shared that he had come in ninth place overall that day. It seemed like a respectable finish. I was in the midst of congratulating him when my husband piped up, "Ben, aren't you going to tell Mom the rest of the story?" Of course I was wondering what details from the story had been omitted. My husband went on to say that Ben had been in third place most of the race—until he lost one of his shoes in the mud about a quarter of a mile from the finish. Yes, Ben ran the last quarter mile of the race in one shoe. And instead of capturing third place, he finished ninth.

This experience had particular significance for Ben. He is an eleven-year-old sixth grader in middle school, and he continues to be challenged in the area of shoe tying. I have hounded Ben for years regarding untied shoes and floppy laces.

My immediate response was, "Ben, you have got to learn to tie your shoes!" Ben looked at my husband and said, "See why I didn't want to tell her?" Shortly after this one-shoe finish, Ben learned to tie his shoes properly.

Making Professional Development Relevant and Rigorous

I thought of this story recently when I heard a keynote presentation by Dr. Willard Daggett (2008). Dr. Daggett talked about the importance of "rigor and relevance" in the work we do with students. It wasn't until shoe tying became strongly relevant in Ben's world that he was willing to work through his battle with shoelaces.

As I listened to Dr. Daggett, I couldn't help thinking that the same is true for adult learners—especially new teachers. The Alliance for Excellent Education in 2004 stated that comprehensive induction programs for new teachers should include "ongoing professional development" (13). After listening to Dr. Daggett speak, I started to really examine the ongoing professional development opportunities that we offered to see if they were truly relevant to teachers' immediate needs.

Monthly New-Teacher Meetings

I knew the research that stated the need for new teachers to have ongoing professional development. I had heard Bruce Morgan, Debbie Miller, and Ellin Keene speak at a session in 2007 at the annual National Council of Teachers of English convention about professional development that has made a difference to them. They shared that having time to converse with colleagues was essential to their learning. And on a personal level, I felt new teachers shouldn't wait three years like I did to find a sense of community within a school. It was with these goals in mind—ongoing site-based professional development, opportunities to share with colleagues, and creating a sense of community—that I decided to pull new teachers together on a monthly basis to meet as a group.

I asked my colleague Leslie Lloyd, a third-grade teacher, to cofacilitate these monthly new-teacher group meetings with me. I knew that Leslie was in the trenches of the classroom and would be key in planning professional development that was relevant to the needs of the new staff.

The project on the "Next Generation of Teachers" at the Harvard Graduate School of Education found that "it is at the school site, rather than at the district, where key factors influencing new teachers' experiences converge; it is there that induction efforts should be centered" (Johnson et al. 2001, 4). My district embraces this finding and, as a result, provides new teachers with a monthly release day as part of their induction. They spend the morning of that day doing peer observations (see Chapter 6).

The afternoon is spent meeting as a group with Leslie and me. However, if you are reading this thinking that it is unrealistic to release all of your new teachers on a monthly basis, you should know that if funds became unavailable to us and new teachers were no longer granted release time during the school day, or if we could not find substitutes to cover the classrooms, Leslie and I would continue to find a way to meet with new teachers. We would probably have to schedule our monthly meetings after school for a shorter period of time, but we would find a way to make the meetings happen regardless of funding. It's that important! If we did have to do away with our monthly release days, I would probably recommend that new teachers do a peer observation a month during free prep period and we would do the curriculum-planning component during some of the weekly meetings that I have with new teachers. We would just have to rethink what we would fit in since you can't squeeze all that we cover in a day into an after-school meeting.

The monthly meetings are designed to provide a safe and supportive environment for new teachers to share challenges, ask questions, and look at how the literacy curriculum fits within the big picture of a school year (see Chapter 8). The group is one of inquiry. It's essential to Leslie and me that our time together is productive and that participants find the days meaningful—that sessions are not just more meetings that take teachers away from their classrooms. So often we bombard new teachers with resources and activities but spend little time showing them how these things fit within the big picture of the district's curriculum and a school year. The ultimate goal of our monthly group meeting is to support new teachers as they work to refine their skills and at the same time help them gain insight into big-picture planning so that they start thinking how curriculum fits over a school year. We want participants to see that teaching is more than the delivery of activities: skillful instruction is about thoughtful planning that hinges on the interconnectedness of days, weeks, and months.

Afternoons with a Predictable Structure

New-teacher meetings have a predictable structure. The afternoons are spent as a group, talking about the morning observations, sharing ideas, asking questions, working with curriculum, sharing literacy strategies, and celebrating our successes.

Sample Schedule of New-Teacher Meeting
- Sharing as a Group and Debriefing Peer Observations
- Reflecting on Student Work
- Working with ELA Curriculum
- Reading Workshop
- Word Study
- Writing Workshop
- Correspondence Through Dialogue Journal

The afternoon meetings always start with processing our morning observations. Those observations set the immediate relevant and rigorous context for our learning. As Leslie and I plan the afternoon meetings, we are constantly asking ourselves if the agenda is relevant to the immediate needs of the new teachers.

Through the first few meetings at the beginning of each year, we try to get a sense of the group's strengths and struggles so that we can tailor upcoming sessions to support their needs. The plan is always to let the group teach us what their basic needs are as new teachers. More times than not, we find ourselves short on time and need to adjust the meeting agenda. When this happens, we always ask the new teachers to review the agenda and reprioritize it. (See Figure 5.1 for a sample meeting agenda.)

Materials

Leslie and I start up the group each year with only a few core materials. Each teacher is given a blank journal for correspondence, a journal they can use as a writer's notebook, our chosen professional text for the year, and a three-ring binder to organize resources that will be handed out throughout the year. The binder is given to participants containing only a few key resources, templates for plotting out curriculum, and a few universal organizers used throughout the school in reading and writing workshop. The binder is divided into the following sections:

- Learning Environments
- Reading Workshop
- Writing Workshop
- Word Study
- Blank Templates (Peer Observation, Curriculum Planning)
- ELA Curriculum
- Resources

New-Teacher Group
January

8:30–11:00	Morning Peer Observations
11:00–11:45	Lunch
11:45–2:30	New-Teacher Group Meeting
11:45–12:15	Reconnecting as a Group

    ✓ Debrief classroom observations.

    ✓ Core text: *Still Learning to Read* by Sibberson and Szymusiak (Chapters 3 and 4)

    ✓ Burning issues?

    ✓ Reflecting on student work

12:15–1:15	Reading Workshop

    ✓ Creating a planning menu

1:15–1:45	Writing Workshop

    ✓ Share celebrations and struggles in launching writing workshop in your classroom.

    ✓ Ourselves as writers

        —View videotape clip, "Dude, Listen to This!" by Ralph Fletcher.

        —Generating titles (Strategy of sketching out setting)

        —Mentor text: *Marshfield Dreams* by Ralph Fletcher

1:45–2:15	Curriculum Planning

    ✓ Sketch out a plan for February.

2:15–2:30	Wrap Up/Dialogue Journal

Putting Ideas into Practice

- Continue thinking about how student work informs our instruction.
- Finish planning out February.
- Read Chapter 5 in *Still Learning to Read* for next month.

Figure 5.1
New-Teacher
Meeting
Agenda

    The idea is that the binder will gradually fill with literacy resources throughout the year. We have new teachers take part in the process of building their own binder so that it will be purposeful and meaningful to them.

    Leslie and I provide the group with various resources that connect to our learning throughout the year. For example, this past year Christine wanted to create her own list of mentor texts and asked Leslie and me to share our favorite ones. We shared the same book, *Dory Story* by Jerry Pallotta, as an example of a mentor text that we had both used with students to demonstrate the concept of a surprise ending, and we gave each teacher a copy. When we introduce a resource to the group, we try to supply the teachers with it so that they have the materials to try out the idea on their own in their classrooms. We don't have a lot of funds, but we do try to set aside about one thousand dollars to buy materials that will support the transfer and implementation of ideas and strategies into the classroom. Here are some of the resources we have given out in the past.

- **Student-Sized Dry Erase Boards**
  While watching a video on word-study strategies, the idea of having students use dry erase boards came up. We bought each teacher a class set of dry erase boards so that they could put the idea into practice.
- **Microcassette Recorders**
  We spent a session talking about reading fluency and various strategies to get students to self-assess their oral reading. The idea was shared of having students record themselves reading and then listen to and self-assess that reading over the course of the year. We were able to buy each teacher six cassette recorders to get started on this strategy.
- **Mentor Texts**
  Two of the new teachers asked Leslie and me if we would share our favorite mentor texts, so we started incorporating one per meeting group. After sharing the book, we would then give each teacher a copy of it to add to their own collection.
- **Books to Add to Classroom Libraries**
  We want new teachers to have classroom libraries that are rich and plentiful, filled with new and enticing books. Leslie and I use bonus points from the book orders to get extra books and then give new teachers piles of them to add to their classroom libraries.
- **Writer's Notebooks**
  Leslie and I always incorporate writing workshop into our sessions. We know that it is not always feasible to buy fancy writer's notebooks for students. One of our favorite resources is from Bare Books. These hardcover blank journals are cheap and can be personalized. They work well as writer's notebooks. We have given teachers in the group a class set of these journals so that they could implement writer's notebooks with students.
- **Sticky Notes and Highlighters**
  Leslie and I shared the strategy on how we can support students to hold their thinking while reading by pausing to jot notes. After having new teachers try out this strategy themselves, we supplied a variety of sticky notes and highlighters so that they too could try this strategy with students.

Reconnecting: A Time to Share

As I've mentioned, we start each afternoon meeting talking about our morning observations. Linguist Michael Halliday wrote: "Language is the essential condition of knowing, the process by which experience becomes knowledge" (1993, 94). It would be easy to cut this talk time out of our agenda since we are so pressed for time, but this is when teachers are able to discuss and process their learning as Leslie and I listen. By listening to their conversations and taking notes, we get a feel for the needs and future direction of the group and a sense of what is relevant to them as learners.

We have found that more times than not, our conversations seem to center on student behaviors. I don't find this surprising since so often it is student behaviors that are challenging new teachers. An example of this is the day one of the new teachers told about watching a student do his own thing—reading a book as she was modeling a strategy for the class. When she leaned over and asked the student what he was doing, he replied, "I just have to know what happens at the end of the book." This situation launched us into a discussion about what we expect as teachers. Would we allow that child to read on? Or do we expect all students to have eyes on us? In the end, we talked about how often we may back students into corners with our own expectations and that sometimes it is okay to let a student finish a book—although we were not all in agreement on this as a group, and that, too, is okay.

Leslie and I asked the group to look at themselves over the next month and think about the things we had just discussed: What is it that you expect of students while you lead lessons? Do you expect all eyes on you as you speak? What about students who are doodling as they listen? Do you allow students to kneel in their chairs, or do you expect all students to sit quietly with their feet on the floor? What do you say to students who are turned around and not facing forward? And do your expectations ever back students into corners? What can we let go of as teachers? We are not looking to come to a consensus as a group but rather to raise thought-provoking situations that allow us to continue to reflect on and solidify what we believe as educators. It is through our conversations that Leslie and I hope that new teachers will gain the insight needed to establish their behavioral ground rules.

At times I find myself wanting to jump into the conversation and share what I think are words of wisdom, but I have learned over time to resist the temptation and that it's more important that I sit back and listen to the learning and inquiries.

Reading Workshop: Working with Curriculum

One of our goals is for the new teachers to become more familiar with curriculum expectations. At one of the earlier meetings in the year, I had shared with the group that I had recently worked with a teacher in her fifth year of teaching who is still struggling to put the pieces together for her reading workshop and that we had spent an afternoon creating a one-page reading workshop menu that she could use to support her planning. The menu was organized by literary concepts, graphic organizers, comprehension strategies, and skills all tailored to third-grade curriculum. The new teachers loved this menu. Leslie and I asked them if they wanted time to create a menu that would support their planning of reading workshop. We shared that the power of the menu was in the process of going through the documents and personalizing it—that it was not something you could just copy, that its power actually lay in the time spent creating it.

The new teachers said that they wanted the time to try this out on their own. We put aside an hour in our schedule so that they could get started. It was exciting to see them take their laptops, literacy notebooks, and new-teacher binders and work together in grade-level teams to create reading workshop menus. Christine worked with Page, who is in her second year of teaching. After they put together their drafted menu (see Figure 5.2), they proudly e-mailed their fourth-grade teaching team, attaching the document they had created.

It was a chance for them to give back. They were thrilled to be able to contribute to their teaching team, a team that had been supporting them throughout the year as new teachers.

Mini-Lesson Ideas

The following reading workshop lesson ideas are the ones we've incorporated into new-teacher groups over the years.

Literature Discussions

We often want teachers to experience the same practices that they are trying to implement in their classrooms and will bring in short text, read it at group, and have our own literature discussions. Some of our favorite text pieces have been commentaries by Rick Reilly that were published in *Sports Illustrated*. At the end of the discussions we will then process what we want our literature discussions in our own classrooms to look like.

First Draft of Reading Workshop Planning Menu Created by Christine and Page

E-mail to Grade 4 Teaching Team

Hi Everyone,

Page and I worked on creating a list (two pages) of skills and concepts that need to be covered in reading workshop. These were taken from our curriculum, fourth-grade skills sheets, and word-study books. We hope this is a helpful tool to pull for mini-lessons for your reading groups. Use or toss, whichever works for you. ☺

Christine

Literary Concepts

- Fluency (phrasing, expression, rate)
- Distinguishes fact from opinion
- States main ideas
- Determines cause and effect
- Summarizes
- Identifies and uses nonfiction text features
- Reads variety of genres (fiction, nonfiction, drama, poetry, biography)
- Identifies major and minor characters
- Compares and contrasts characters
- Identifies character traits
- Identifies beg-mid-end of story
- Identifies literary devices (figurative language and symbolism)
- Identifies and explains themes in text
- Poetry (rhyme, rhythm, alliteration, onomatopoeia)
- Uses informational text features (bold words, headings, illustrations, maps, charts, bullets)
- Identifies purpose of persuasive text

Skills

- Singular and plural possessives
- Prefixes (*pre, dis, bi, tri, sub, anti, trans*)
- Suffixes (*ment, ous, ty, tion, ward, ent, ish, ness*)
- Root words
- Double vowels where each vowel has its own sound (*duel, idiom, create, poet, idea*)
- Different letter combos represent same sounds (*nation, ocean, show, machine, laugh, phone*)
- Syllables
- Glossary skills
- Dictionary skills (guide words, pronunciation, appropriate meaning)
- Variety of sources for research
- Patterns from word-study books

Graphic Organizers

- FQR
- Reading response
- Sticky notes
- Character traits
- Venn diagram
- Vocabulary sheets
- Illustrator page
- Story board (cumulative summary)
- Biography organizer
- Theme organizer

Comprehension Strategies (Before, During, and After Reading)

- Establish purpose
- Recall sequence of events
- Hold thinking (sticky notes, key words)
- Apply thinking (discussion, response)

Read for Meaning:

- Makes inferences (reads between the lines)
- Makes connections (That reminds me of, Remember when)
- Asks questions (I wonder, How come, I'm confused)
- Visualizes (I can see it, I get a picture in my mind)
- Determines important info (This is really important, Why is this important)
- Synthesizes info (brings it all together)
- Repairing understanding (This doesn't make sense)

Figure 5.2

Reading with a Purpose

We often include adult literature in our group meetings. If we want to model reading with a purpose, we will use adult literature to do so. We have used the book *The Glass Castle: A Memoir* by Jeannette Walls. For this exercise we ask the teachers to read the back cover and first couple of pages of the book and, as they read, to jot down on a sticky note character names that they encounter and any wonderings that they might have.

Reading Response

We will also ask participants in the group to respond to a piece of text through writing. If we expect students to communicate their thinking through writing, it is important that we do so too, using adult literature. Having new teachers write a response fosters an awareness of our own processes as readers and what we do as readers and writers to organize and access our thinking about texts that we read.

Writing Workshop: Modeling by Example

Leslie and I also integrate practical strategies that can be transferred to both the reading and the writing workshop. Instead of just talking about these workshops, we want to model by example.

One of the challenges that had been shared by several teachers is how to get students to generate ideas for writing stories. I had modeled in several of their classrooms the strategy of sketching out a setting map as a way to get students thinking about stories. Leslie and I wanted to take this idea further and have teachers try out this strategy themselves in their writer's notebook. The first thing we did was show them a video excerpt from "Dude, Listen to This!" In this clip, Ralph Fletcher models the strategy with a group of fourth graders. The clip was of particular interest to the teachers since the video was shot at our school. After watching the video, I shared my own setting map of my childhood house in Vermont and the titles of stories that I generated from the map. (See Figure 5.3 for my setting map and Figure 5.4 for an outline of the writing workshop schedule for the day.) We then had the teachers try out this strategy on their own.

Throughout the experience you could sense the teachers developing their own visions and thoughts on how they wanted to integrate or refine writing workshop within their own classrooms. Christine was excited to share her map and stories with the group. She said that she

Figure 5.3
Jen's Setting
Map: Growing
Up in Vermont

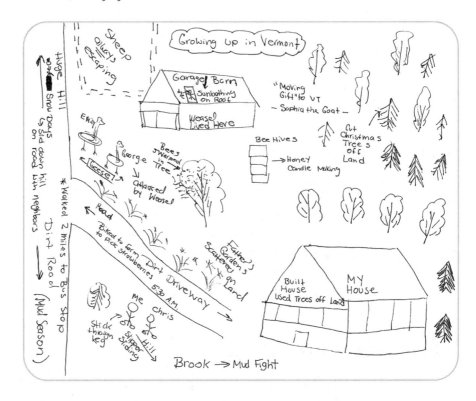

saw the value of doing this activity herself and that she will share this map and her thinking with students when she introduces the idea as a mini-lesson next year.

We want new teachers to have the resources to implement ideas shared within the group. To help support the transfer and application of this strategy, we gave each teacher in the group a copy of *How to Write Your Life Story* by Ralph Fletcher and pointed out that the idea for sketching out the setting map came from this book. So now the teachers had the resources to try this idea on their own.

Mini-Lesson Ideas

The following writing workshop lesson ideas are ones that we've incorporated into new-teacher groups over the years.

Generating Titles

At the beginning of each year we give new teachers a journal that they can use as a writer's notebook. We spend time generating and writing down titles of stories that we might want to write about someday.

> ## WRITING WORKSHOP AFTERNOON SEGMENT
>
> - **Videotape Excerpt**
>   Viewed videotape excerpt from "Dude, Listen to This!" In this excerpt Ralph Fletcher models the strategy of sketching out a setting to generate titles with a class of fourth-grade students.
>
> - **Mentor Text**
>   Leslie and I read the short story "Jimmy" from Ralph Fletcher's book *Marshfield Dreams: When I Was a Kid.* This book has a setting map on the inside cover, and teachers had copies of it so that they could see the map referenced in the short story.
>
> - **Ourselves as Writers**
>   We then had everyone in the group try out this strategy of sketching out a setting map and generating titles for potential stories that they can write about throughout the year.
>
> - **Resource**
>   We bought each teacher a paperback copy of Ralph's book *How to Write Your Life Story.* This is the book where Leslie and I found the idea of sketching out a setting as a strategy for generating titles.

Figure 5.4

Ourselves as Writers

We often have teachers write snapshots about their own lives. Writing is hard. It is hard for teachers as well as for kids. It is important that we experience the process that we ask our students to go through.

Mentor Texts

The teachers love learning about new mentor texts. In talking about having students write narratives, it came up that students struggle with creating believable characters. We spent time as a group looking through picture books and finding mentor texts in which authors have established a well-defined character. The Scaredy Squirrel and Chester books by Melanie Watt were among our favorites!

Dialogue Journals

Leslie and I want all participants to have a voice. We recognize that some are more verbal than others, so we end each session by having participants reflect in a dialogue journal. Dialogue journals support relationship building—they are an informal channel that facilitates communication. Exchanging journals is another opportunity for less verbal participants to share their thinking, and the written responses provide us as facilitators with insight into participants' reflections. Leslie and I both respond to the teachers, providing a timely response and returning their journals within a day or two.

Ideas for Journaling Prompts
- What have you tried since our last meeting?
- What are you wondering about this week?
- What are some unanticipated roadblocks or challenges?
- What's working well in your classroom?
- What would you still like to implement?
- Do you have any student success stories you would like to share?

The dialogue journal also helps us keep a pulse on how new teachers are feeling about the group and the relevance of the professional development that we had planned for the afternoon. As you can see in Christine's entry, she found the time spent creating a planning menu for reading workshop with Page to be time well spent.

Christine's January Dialogue Journal Entry

I enjoyed having time to put together the menu for reading workshop. That will be helpful for pulling ideas quickly for mini-lessons at group time. The mapping was good also, so I can see if I'm on track.

While watching the students, I found myself relating the students' level of engagement to what the teacher was doing and the distribution of time for the lesson.

It would be great to have a list of literacy concepts and mentor texts that go with each one. I know a few, but could use some new ideas.

Keeping It Simple

A few years ago I read an article by Juli Kendall in *Journal of Staff Development*. In it, she wrote, "Written on a sticky note stuck to the edge of my laptop are three phrases: Listen first; teach by example; be patient. These are three things I've learned as a school-based literacy coach" (2007, 76). Her words often swim around in my head as Leslie and I cram to get through our afternoon group meetings with the new teachers.

I often have to remember to listen to what the teachers are telling us, to sit back and hear their successes, and to support their individual learning curves. It is so easy to be tempted to cut conversations short and want to move on down the planned agenda.

Juli's quote also reminds me that I need to be patient. Learning takes time, and it never happens as quickly as I would like. Sometimes I forget about all the other curricular demands that a new teacher has to juggle beyond literacy. I forget how hard it was for me as a new teacher to incorporate all of my new learning into the classroom.

It's hard being a new teacher. It's hard being an effective literacy coach. We all want to feel successful. We also both need to remember that learning takes time, as adults, and as children.

I know Leslie and I will still need reminders on where we should focus our time and energy, that less is more, and—as my son, Ben, has reminded me through his challenge with shoe tying—that relevance is the key in working with new teachers. If the professional development is not relevant to their immediate needs, chances are the learning won't transfer.

So I, too, have taped a sticky note to my computer, with Juli's words to guide me: "Listen first; teach by example; be patient." Because it is my hope that by having these new teachers meet monthly as a group they will refine their skills and begin to feel like an integral part of our school community—and at the end of each day; at the end of each month; and, ultimately, at the finish line, the end of the year, they will still feel they have made the right choice by working at our school and will be proud to be part of the teaching profession.

CHAPTER SIX

Peer Observations

*Making our practice mutually visible will never be easy, because
we will never be fully confident that we know what we're
supposed to be doing and that we're doing it well. And we're
never quite sure just how students will behave. None of us want
to be exposed as incompetent. Yet there is no more powerful way
of learning and improving on the job than by observing others
and having others observe us.*

ROLAND BARTH, 2006

Years ago a group of us from school received a teacher research grant
from the Spencer Foundation. Our grant project explored the impact
teacher research groups had on the instructional practices of teachers and
on student achievement. For three years, we met regularly as a group, and
talked throughout our workdays as we followed individual and small-
group teacher inquiries. It was really my first experience being part of a
professional learning community. The grant enabled us to saturate ourselves in professional development—opportunities that we felt were essential to our learning. We designed our budget to include money to attend
the annual NCTE conference, purchase professional texts, participate in a
research retreat, and hire substitutes so that we could be released to do
peer observations.

One of the greatest outcomes of the teacher research group was an increased sense of collegiality. Teachers felt that the group gave them a supportive learning community where ideas were freely given and taken as well as a renewed passion and energy for teaching.

But would you believe that even with this outcome of increased collegiality, we spent every cent of that grant except the line earmarked for our classroom observations of one another? Not one of us involved in the grant touched that budget line. It was not that it was just ignored or forgotten, but as teachers we were insecure about going into other classrooms or hosting colleagues for many reasons, and the grant was proof that we were not as ready as we thought we were to do this. It wasn't until I started working as a literacy coach and going into classrooms on a daily basis that I began to see just how much we could learn from spending time in each other's classrooms.

One of my first observations was of Maxine, a veteran fifth-grade teacher. As I walked into Maxine's room I was immediately comforted by the warm, inviting learning environment. Right away I noticed a couch for students to work at, plants along the windowsill, and a rug in the meeting area. Framed prints by artists such as Vermeer and Van Gogh that Maxine had collected on her travels abroad hung on the walls. As I watched her wrap up a morning class meeting, I was struck by the sense of community that was established. What I remember seeing were relaxed students sitting quietly on the rug and on the couch. What I remember hearing were twenty students eloquently reciting from memory "Stopping by Woods on a Snowy Evening" by Robert Frost. I can still hear the young voices performing in unison with feeling and emotion: "Whose woods these are I think I know . . ." The moment brought goose bumps. I remember thinking, What a powerful and effective way to reinforce oral reading fluency. I knew right then and there that I could learn a lot from Maxine. And over the years I have continued to visit her room on a regular basis and still continue to learn from her. I know one thing for sure: Maxine has a gift for embedding literacy instruction within authentic and meaningful learning contexts for her students. Meaningful literacy instruction is present throughout the day and spreads to all corners of her room.

Getting Started with Peer Observations

Once I had experienced the power of classroom observation myself, I began to think about how I could incorporate observations into new-teacher induction.

Peer observations were a new experience not only for the new teachers but also for the veteran teachers who were being observed. In the beginning, Leslie and I approached classroom teachers and asked if they would be willing to be observed by a new teacher. We were surprised by how many teachers declined this offer! But in thinking back to Barth's quote at the start of this chapter (and to my Spencer Foundation experience), it all made sense; we should not have been surprised. Many of us, myself included, are insecure in our own teaching. We are hesitant to have others watch us. But as Barth points out, "There is no more powerful way of learning and improving on the job than by observing others and having others observe us" (2006, 12). Although the observations were not exactly embraced by those being observed in the beginning, enough teachers did open their doors so that we could move forward. And as the veteran teachers realized how much the new teachers appreciated being able to learn from them (thank-you notes worked wonders), more doors started to open. In hindsight, what we should have done prior to implementation of these observations was to talk with the full staff about the purpose behind peer observations and explain how this was an opportunity for new teachers to see the strengths that we all possess—and that the observations were an authentic learning opportunity.

After arranging the initial new-teacher observations, Leslie and I quickly decided to shift this responsibility to the new teachers themselves. We stepped back from setting up peer observations because we wanted new teachers to self-reflect on their own needs and set their own purpose for their observations. It was probably a smart move that Leslie and I decided not to put ourselves in the middle of directing this. Who were we to judge whom the new teachers should be observing or whom they would learn the most from?

Four years later, Leslie and I are surprised at how comfortable new teachers are at setting up their own observations. We are equally surprised at how well received they are by the veteran teachers. I don't think a new teacher has ever been turned away from observing in another teacher's room. Veteran teachers welcome the new teachers into their room and openly share ideas with them. New teachers walk away with a renewed sense of optimism and concrete ideas they can bring back and try in their own classrooms.

How do the new teachers even know whom to observe? Many new teachers will start off the year by observing the mentor who has been assigned to them through the school's governing board. (The school-based mentor is part of the state's certification process.) Leslie and I have also noticed that the second-year teachers in the group will usually offer suggestions and guide the first-year teachers to classrooms that they might enjoy observing.

Monthly Observations

Peer observations are now a well-established practice for new teachers within our school. These observations are part of the structured release that includes the afternoon monthly meeting as mentioned in Chapter 5 and are the base of the discussions for that meeting. It is crucial that new teachers not only have opportunities to observe others teaching but also have time to come together with their peers and talk about what they have seen.

Veteran teachers are proud to be part of this process. At a recent staff meeting one of the teachers (with seven years' experience) praised the new-teacher induction and went on to say, "I am only jealous that I didn't start off my teaching with the same level of support!"

Observation Forms

Leslie and I have developed a few observation forms to help new teachers focus their viewing during an observation and serve as a tool to launch discussions. These forms have evolved over time and have gone through several revisions with input from the new teachers themselves.

The observation forms are simple and were designed so that they wouldn't intimidate the observer or the teacher being observed. Leslie and I knew that we could have created more comprehensive forms, ones filled with various specific criteria under all of the headings that we did come up with, but we were cautious of littering our forms with too much information that may have little meaning. We didn't want to create a checklist on which they could just check off what they might have seen; instead, we wanted to flip it around and have them actually generate on the form what they saw in the classroom. The observation forms were designed to ensure that the teachers shared common elements in their observations.

Two-Column Notes Form

The first observation form that we ask new teachers to use is the two-column notes form with the headings What I Notice and What I Might Try in My Classroom (Figure 6.1; also in appendix). This form is an invitation.

Two-Column Notes Form

What I Notice	What I Might Try in My Classroom

Figure 6.1

It sets new teachers up from the start to look for ideas that they can take away from the observation and try in their own classroom.

At the start of the school year Christine observed a morning meeting of another fourth-grade teacher, Stacy. Christine was interested in observing Stacy's morning meeting based on the Responsive Classroom and wanted to glean new insight into class meeting time in hopes of being able to take away a few ideas that she could incorporate into her own class meeting. During the observation, Christine watched Stacy's class participate in their morning meeting routine. She sat in on the class as they discussed qualities of a good handshake greeting. Christine wrote on her observation notes that this was a conversation she would like to have with her own students. She also noticed that Stacy allocated time for the class to talk about student comments that were added to the morning message. Christine noted on her two-column notes sheet that she might want to try incorporating the morning message back into the meeting time with the kids.

Observation Notes Form

The second form that we use, the observation notes form, outlines the different target areas of instruction that we want the teachers to zone in on (Figure 6.2; also in appendix).

OBSERVATION NOTES FORM

Teacher: _____ **Date:** _____

Sketch the room on the back.

Focus of Lesson:

Zone in On . . .	Distribution of Time	What Do You Notice?	What Do You Wonder?	What Might You Like to Try?
Teacher (What is the teacher doing?)				
Evidence of Gradual Release				
Student Engagement (What are the students doing?)				
Materials				
Environment				
Assessment (How do you know the students are getting it?)				

Figure 6.2

Target Areas
- Teacher
  What is the teacher doing?
- **Evidence of Gradual Release**
  What is the instructional bridge from the teacher demonstration to the independent student practice?

- **Student Engagement**
  What are the students doing?
- **Materials**
  What materials are being used?
- **Environment**
  How would you describe the learning environment? What do you see?
  What do you hear?
- **Assessment**
  How do you know the students are getting it?

Within each target area, we ask teachers to think about time distribution, what they notice, what they wonder, and what they might like to try. This is the same form that teachers take notes on when they are observing me (see Chapter 2). The form evolved over the first year of implementing the observations. One issue that we ran into in trying to limit it to only one page was lack of space for certain things. We ask teachers to sketch the layout of the room. They shared that they liked sketching it out, but many needed more space than we had provided on the front of the observation page. So now most teachers will sketch the desk arrangement on the front of the form but will then turn it over and actually do a more in-depth sketch of the room on the back. We also added a box for teachers to focus in on gradual release. We talk about gradual release, but do we know what it looks like when we see it in the classroom? We wanted to help new teachers look for the bridge between teacher modeling and independent student practice. The hope is that the observation form is functional and informal and yet serves as a vehicle that guides conversations about literacy instruction. Even though we ask teachers to focus in on specific instructional target areas, our hope is that the form fosters self-reflection and that observers weigh what they are seeing against their own teaching styles and classrooms.

Most of the teachers have found that the observation notes form helps focus their observations. Some teachers prefer to take notes in a notebook and then go back and plot out and organize their thinking on the form. All agree that they love the sections to write down what they might try out in their classroom and the space to jot down their wonderings. Peter Johnston refers to an "I wonder" as a "linguistic lubricant." He further explains in his book *Choice Words*, "It marks the offering of possible hypothesis, or a tentative idea with an invitation but not an insistence, to pick up and improve it or take it further" (2004, 68).

Learning from a Not-So-Great Observation: Jessica

Lessons don't always work out completely as planned! That's the reality of teaching. Jessica got to experience this firsthand. She had arranged to observe reading workshop in Carolyn's fourth-grade classroom. It just so happened that on that particular day, I was actually coteaching with Carolyn during Jessica's observation, so I too had the dubious pleasure of experiencing the lesson firsthand. Carolyn and I had way too much planned. Not only were we planning to launch student-led discussions but we were also planning to introduce students to a triple Venn diagram, all within a forty-five-minute period. We realized early on in the lesson that the students needed more support in leading their own discussions. They struggled within their small groups to have a responsive conversation and were talking to each other, not with each other. Students were simply going in a circle and reading their sticky notes that held their thinking out loud to the group. Their comments were unconnected and not at all what we had envisioned for our student-led discussions. As Carolyn and I observed the student groups, we could see that the children were still unsure of the purpose for a literature discussion.

Jessica got to see how Carolyn and I modified our original plan in the midst of reading workshop to better meet the needs of the students. Jess watched as we ditched our plans to introduce the Venn diagram and instead spent the entire reading workshop focusing in on the literature discussions. After the student discussion groups, we pulled the children back together as a class and revisited our expectations for literature discussions. We then asked students to reflect on what went well in their discussions and what they still needed to work on.

When Jessica and I debriefed the observation, she shared that she realized that she too was trying to fit way too much into them and that it was important for her to rethink the purpose of her lessons to maximize learning. But at the same time, it was hard not to keep plowing through lessons since she felt pressure to keep up with other fourth-grade teachers. On her observation form she wrote, "My original idea for my literature circles now seems a little 'too much.' Why not keep it simple and focus on one thing—character—to build confidence and set procedures for literature circles." By observing the reading workshop in action and this not-so-great lesson, Jessica realized it was okay to take a few steps back and rethink reading and writing workshop—that it is important to maintain quality over quantity.

Debriefing Peer Observations

New teachers are able to chat with the host teacher for a few minutes during their actual observation time. They also have an opportunity to share their observations with and debrief one another during our group meetings. (See Chapter 5, Figure 5.1, for the new-teacher group meeting agenda.) Debriefing gives teachers the opportunity to share their reflections and new insights with the other new teachers.

In the beginning of the year we find that many of our debrief conversations revolve around room arrangement, behavior-management plans, and organizational systems. In the group debrief that followed one of her recent observations in Stacy's room, Christine shared that she is amazed by Stacy's management and transitions. You can see Christine's thinking in the following notes taken from her observation form:

- Surprising how quiet they are since they are in table groups.
- How do you keep independent workers so quiet and focused?
- I want to encourage my students to share their thinking more freely.
- Good transitions.
- How do you get both a discussion and a mini-lesson in such a short time?

Christine initiated our group debrief by saying, "First of all no one was pirouetting across the room! I would love to know how Stacy gets this all in place and how I am going to get it all in place at the beginning of next year." Page, a second-year teacher, responded, "I feel your pain. The classroom I have is not the classroom I have envisioned. I feel powerless." This honest, raw conversation continued among the group. What was communicated was their understanding that behavior management is interfering with their ability to really focus in on and refine their instructional strategies. But they all were committed to continuing to push through the pain and continuing to take on the challenge of behavior management. Page and Christine closed the conversation by sharing that they would revisit transition time within their classrooms and that they would go back to Stacy and talk with her more about what she did with her students in the beginning of the year to establish these smooth transitions in the classroom.

As the year progresses, the conversation tends to shift to time distribution and instruction. Teachers gain interesting insights on time distribution within a lesson. Christine shared that she watched a teacher break down a forty-five-minute lesson into fifteen-minute chunks of time and that students were engaged in learning for the full forty-five minutes. She thought this might be a more effective strategy for her group than simply providing a mini-lesson and having her students work independently for the next thirty-five minutes. It was then that another new teacher within the group piggybacked on the concept of mini-lessons and shared a personal reflection that she realized that her mini-lessons weren't so "mini" and were taking too long. She wanted to rethink the way she distributes time within her own lessons. The focus on time and how it is used by so many of the new teachers is interesting. It is something concrete, easy for a new teacher to hold on to—they can literally watch the clock and see where and when the instruction moves or shifts, which is much easier to do than to notice some of the subtleties of great teaching.

Peer Observations in Year Two and Beyond

Teachers in their second year of new-teacher induction and those who are beyond tend to be very purposeful when setting up peer observations and go into the observation with a specific goal in mind, usually working to refine an established practice.

After several years of teaching, Lucy was still interested in management but in a more sophisticated way. It wasn't about keeping a lid on kids, but rather, setting up a structure where her students could be truly independent and she could have higher expectations for what they would accomplish during writing workshop. She felt she needed to develop a better system of keeping track of where students were in the writing process. She was still overwhelmed with working out the nuts and bolts of writing workshop, so she set up two classroom observations. One was of Leslie (a veteran teacher) and the other was of Jessica (a newer teacher). Lucy went into her observations with the specific purpose of looking for a management strategy. During the observations, she picked up the idea of incorporating status of the class (Atwell 1998) into her writing workshop. She saw this idea implemented in slightly different ways in the two classrooms.

In the first observation, Lucy saw Leslie using a more traditional status-of-the-class check sheet with students' names already written on the form (see Figure 6.3; also in appendix). She watched how Leslie checked in with each student, finding out where he or she was working within the writing process. Lucy then watched this same idea implemented by Jessica, who had adapted the status-of-the-class sheet to create a magnetic status-of-the-class board (see Figure 6.4). The magnetic board involved students in the process by having them place their names on it. For example, if students

Status-of-the-Class Form

Students	Genre	Peer Conference	Revision	Teacher Edit	Final Draft	Teacher Observations

Figure 6.3

Figure 6.4
Jessica's
Magnetic
Status-of-the-
Class Board

needed a teacher edit, they would take their laminated names (backed by magnetic tape) and move them under "Teacher Edit." This way Jessica could always look up at the board and see where students were within the writing process.

At the end of the observations, Lucy shared that she wanted to try out both of these ideas in her own classroom. She saw the benefit of Leslie's method of having a hard copy that showed where her students were working within the writing process on a daily basis, and she also liked Jessica's take on the status of the class using the magnetic board. Lucy loved the idea that she would be able to see where her students were by just glancing up during workshop time.

Group Observations

When we first incorporated peer observations into new-teacher induction, we had teachers do solo observations. As observing in classrooms became more of an accepted practice within our school, and veteran staff was more comfortable being observed, we began playing with various groupings of observations. New teachers began to go into classrooms with a partner or as a group.

This past fall we did a group observation during one of Leslie's reading workshops. As we walked into the room, we were greeted by the upbeat rhythmic sounds of Jack Johnson's song "Upside Down" from the Curious George sound track and watched the third-grade students quietly transition from putting away morning work to taking out materials for reading workshop. I saw students smiling and grooving along to the music as they organized themselves to start reading workshop. During this classroom observation, the five of us in the group watched Leslie masterfully orchestrate her reading workshop, rotating through and facilitating three different literature groups as the rest of the class worked independently. We were able to watch her seamless transitions between literature groups as she touched base with individual students. What struck us was that Leslie didn't need to do much talking. Routines were established within the room, and students knew exactly what was expected of them. All she said was, "I am ready for the Mr. Putter and Tabby group." We then observed the group that was reading *Class Clown* by Johanna Hurwitz go back to their seats and continue reading as six other students gathered their reading notebooks and *Mr. Putter and Tabby Pick the Pears* (Rylant 1995) and joined Leslie at the round table. I asked one of Leslie's students how she liked the book she was reading. Without further prompting, she went on to tell me, "Mrs. Lloyd is a great teacher. It's not all about learning. She makes sure that we have a little fun every day. Do you want me to show you how we do our morning meeting?" I found this to be just one example of how Leslie's students are clear on routines and expectations. And most importantly, they are all having fun while learning within their classroom community.

Having had this shared experience, we were then able to talk about the observation and what we noticed later that afternoon as a group. We had all noticed how Leslie maximized instructional time evidenced by fitting in three literature groups during a forty-five-minute time frame, that her students all knew expectations and engaged in sustained reading independently, and that Leslie did not lose any time during transitions. This group observation pushed us all to reflect on the internal structures that we have set up within our own reading workshop and to ask ourselves how we could continue to work to maximize instructional time with students while decreasing time lost in transitions.

Having a group of teachers or even a pair observe a lesson is a good way to mix up peer observations. Christine and Page had observed in Stacy's room together. I think that is why they had such a rich conversation regarding her behavior management and transition times. By observing with another peer, new teachers not only have the opportunity to observe the practice but also have a shared experience with colleagues in analyzing what they've seen.

Embracing the Power of Observation

New teachers have paved the way for peer observations among all staff within our school. Veteran teachers are also getting in on the observation action. After Maxine was recently observed by a new teacher, she immediately went to the principal and asked if she could have a professional day to observe that same teacher. She commented, "I really need to get out of my classroom. I think I could really learn something new from Sadie. Just from talking to her I know she has something special going on with her students."

When new teachers are looking to explore a new idea, they think nothing of setting up a time to observe another teacher during a special or planning period. As a first-year teacher, Christine is already fitting in extra peer observations driven by her own motives during her free prep periods. The other day she shared that she was going to visit Stacy's room for a science lesson since she really needed to see how another teacher introduced the sound unit to students.

These monthly peer observations have become one of the most powerful components of our new-teacher support. The fact that they are built into the school calendar, and are part of the regular school day, communicates the message that observing peers is an important part of our school culture. New teachers are establishing lifelong habits of collaboration and reflection through these observations. Most importantly, new teachers have the opportunity to witness firsthand the many unique gifts that their fellow teachers possess.

CHAPTER SEVEN

Using Student Work to Guide Instruction

Robust learning generally requires robust teaching, and both diagnostic and formative assessments, or assessments for learning, are catalysts for better teaching. In the end, however, when assessment is seen as learning—for students as well as for teachers—it becomes most informative and generative for students and teachers alike.

CAROL ANN TOMLINSON, 2007/2008

By January, we were approximately halfway through the school year. Christine and I had a well-established routine of meeting Monday afternoons. We often used this time to plan and look through student work.

I realized that we hadn't looked through any of her students' reading responses together since last fall. There is always so much to fit into our weekly meetings that unfortunately it is easy for an instructional piece to slip from the radar.

I asked Christine to grab Jacob's reading notebook. I was especially interested in looking at his notebook since he was someone who had been a puzzle to us since the start of the year. I sensed that he was not working to potential and that we as teachers were not getting everything out of him as a student. And, on second thought, I asked her to bring a stack of other

*Figure 7.1
Jacob's
Response to
Tales of a
Fourth Grade
Nothing*

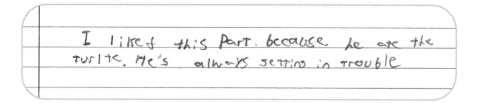

students' reading notebooks so that we could look at her class as a whole and get a feel for Jacob in relation to his peers.

At our meeting, Christine pulled out Jacob's reading notebook. She flipped to his last reading response. It was a concluding response to the book *Tales of a Fourth Grade Nothing* by Judy Blume. I remember thinking that his response looked the same as the first one that he had written earlier in the year, not the type of response we would expect from a fourth-grade student (see Figure 7.1).

Jacob's response was two sentences long, without any mention of the title of the book he was reading or the characters that he was writing about. I wasn't completely surprised. Even though he was such a smart kid, he was a very reluctant writer and didn't communicate all that he understood about the books that he read.

Christine started showing me responses from other students (see Figure 7.2 for a sample response), and they all looked the same—just like Jacob's.

I didn't know what to do or say; I just sat there as Christine went from notebook to notebook. My stomach began to sink. Another feature that caught my eye was the numbers along the margins of some of the responses. Instead of writing the response in paragraph form, the students had literally written a sentence on each line and numbered the lines.

Figure 7.2

SAMPLE STUDENT RESPONSE TO *Stink*

Response Question:
What is your favorite part in this chapter? Use evidence to support your thinking.

Student Response:
1. I liked this part because Webster was a grump.
2. Later in the chapter he finds out it was because Stink didn't go to Webster's party.

As I looked at the responses, I had no sense of what they were writing about or what they had been reading. I also noticed that the students had not been redirected in this practice. I wondered what Christine thought a reading response should look like. Were these responses acceptable to her?

What was most upsetting to me was that the responses from the lowest-performing students were not that different from the ones from the highest-performing students—all about a few sentences in length, all lacking developed thinking. A million thoughts went through my mind. Had she been clear with her students in terms of expectations for reading responses? And, if so, were students being held accountable?

Regardless of the instructional breakdown, it was not an option to say or do nothing. I knew that Christine and I could learn from this, and that this would be a learning opportunity for how we would use student work to guide our instruction to get the most out of her students.

But first, let's go back to the beginning of the year.

Talking About Student Work

Assessment doesn't end when teachers turn in their fall data. In fact it actually marks the beginning of the assessment cycle that we engage in as teachers and students throughout the year. Once diagnostic assessments are completed and we have a baseline on students (see Chapter 3), we shift our attention to the day-to-day formative assessment that drives our instruction and betters our teaching. And, as Carol Ann Tomlinson points out in her article "Learning to Love Assessment," "Assessments for learning are catalysts for better teaching" (2007/2008, 13).

The support teachers receive through our new-teacher induction is deeply rooted in the belief that student work is the foundational means to guide instruction. We want new teachers to use student work to inform their instruction. We also want to communicate that the best plan is not always moving forward, plowing through curriculum, but rather, ensuring that students understand what has been taught, and that may mean going backward and reteaching concepts already covered—but not learned.

I remember one of my son's teachers making a comment a few years ago regarding a math program. She shared that the class was right where they should be in the book. She went on and said, "This new math program is taking all of the other teachers a lot longer to teach. The other teachers are all behind where they should be. They will never make it through the book." And then, in her next breath, "None of the kids in this room get this math anyways." As a parent, I was not happy. Why would I want my child moving through a math program at the targeted pace if he didn't understand what he was learning? I would rather have Ben end the year behind the targeted unit than not understand any of the concepts taught throughout the year.

This scenario reminded me of my work with new teachers and that I don't want to be marching them through a series of assessments at a certain pace, so much that they lose sight of the greater goal, which is student learning.

Targeted Learning Goals and Student Work

One way in which we support ongoing formative assessment is through the reflection on student work. In their widely referenced article "Inside the Black Box: Raising Standards through Classroom Assessment," Black and Wiliam state that "assessments become formative when the evidence is actually used to adapt teaching to meet student needs" (1998, 140). As a school, we have created a template that we use for reflecting on and talking about student work (see Figure 7.3). New teachers use this template in our weekly meetings and at our new-teacher group meetings.

Figure 7.3

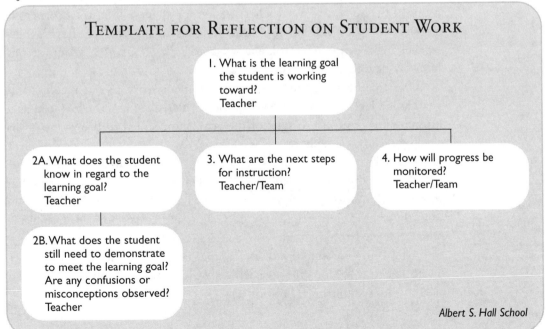

TEMPLATE FOR REFLECTION ON STUDENT WORK

1. What is the learning goal the student is working toward?
Teacher

2A. What does the student know in regard to the learning goal?
Teacher

2B. What does the student still need to demonstrate to meet the learning goal? Are any confusions or misconceptions observed?
Teacher

3. What are the next steps for instruction?
Teacher/Team

4. How will progress be monitored?
Teacher/Team

Albert S. Hall School

Student Work Template

The template is a series of conversational prompts that guide the discussion. The first several questions are intended for the teacher sharing the work, and it is the teacher who sets the focus for what we are looking at in it. The template forces us to ask about the teacher's intended learning goal. Once the learning goal has been identified by the teacher, we then look at the student work to see if the goal has been met. By looking at the work, we identify strengths and needs of the students in relation to the learning goal. We are then able to collaborate and brainstorm ideas for instructional next steps and strategies for monitoring the progress of students we were concerned about.

The language of the template provides a clear framework for teachers to talk about student work. We have found that it serves as a systematic tool that guides our conversations, so that in the end, our reflections impact classroom instruction and benefit those who matter the most—our students.

Reflecting on Student Work as a Group with Christine

Dylan Wiliam writes, "Meeting regularly in teacher learning communities is one of the best ways for teachers to develop their skill in using formative assessment" (2007/2008, 36). Believing this to be true, we have a new teacher bring a piece of student work to talk about as a group at our monthly new-teacher meeting.

Christine brought the first piece of student work to our meeting this year. Since Jacob, whom we met earlier in this chapter, had surfaced as a puzzling kid right at the start of the year, she decided to bring one of his reading responses to share.

Jacob wrote the response while reading the book *Stink: The Incredible Shrinking Kid* by Megan McDonald (see Figure 7.4). Christine told us that this was an emotional chapter and that she had asked students to reflect on how the character of Stink may be feeling and to support their thinking with evidence from the text.

After Christine shared Jacob's reading response and her assignment, we asked her to talk to us more specifically about the learning goals in relation to this assignment (Question 1).

1. What is the learning goal the student is working toward?

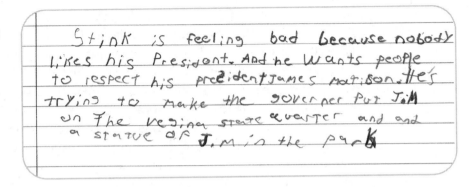

Stink is feeling bad because nobody likes his President. And he wants people to respect his president James matison. He's trying to make the governer put J.M on the vesing state quarter and and a statue of J.M in the park

Why had she assigned this response, and what was she hoping to learn through this work? Christine shared that she wanted Jacob to recognize the character's feelings and communicate a deeper understanding of the text, one that went beyond a literal level.

The next questions (Questions 2A and 2B) go together.

2A. What does the student know in regard to the learning goal?
2B. What does the student still need to demonstrate to meet the learning goal? Are any confusions or misconceptions observed?

The teacher then shares what he or she sees as the strengths and needs of the student in relation to the learning goal. Has the student gotten it? Is there any confusion observed through the work?

Christine said that Jacob identified that he thought Stink was feeling bad, and Jacob was able to articulate it. Another teacher jumped in and questioned whether this wasn't more of a summary than a response and whether this response really communicated a deepened understanding of the story. The group agreed that Jacob did not use evidence from the text to support his thinking but that he is connected to the character on some level.

The essential part of reflecting on the student work lies with the team. The new teachers work together to examine the student work and brainstorm instructional strategies for the student (Question 3).

3.   What are the next steps for instruction?

It is at this point that the teachers look at strategies for reteaching when a student doesn't quite get it and at how to reimmerse students in learning experiences that meet their needs and learning styles.

The team reread Jacob's response and talked about next steps for instruction. They felt that Jacob understood the gist of the story but that he needed to continue to work on communicating his thinking about the story and the characters and use evidence from the text as support. Christine felt that the next steps should support Jacob in helping him to expand his thinking. The team wondered if Jacob had prior experience writing reading responses. Was he clear on what a reading response should include? The team brainstormed some instructional ideas. One teacher suggested that it might help to offer Jacob a graphic organizer such as a character web to hold and organize his thinking prior to writing a reading response. Another idea was to explicitly teach how to use evidence from the text—such as a quote—to support thinking.

Christine liked both ideas given to her by her peers and was eager to go back and model these strategies for the class. She felt that Jacob along with most of her students would benefit from them. In the end, Christine questioned her teaching and wondered if she needed to show her students examples of reading responses.

The key to this whole process is the next question (Question 4):

4. How will progress be monitored?

How will we know when the student "gets it"? The team talks about strategies for monitoring progress.

Christine decided that it would make sense to monitor Jacob's progress through additional reading responses so that she could document his growth over time.

Slow Down, Teach Again, and Provide Models!

So when, in January, we found that Jacob's responses, and those of many of his peers, consisted of limited retellings and didn't demonstrate any deep understanding of the text, we realized that the whole class would benefit from the reteaching of reading responses. Did Christine's students truly understand what a reading response should look and sound like? Had she been clear in her expectations back in the beginning of the year? Had Christine shared examples of other reading responses with her students? In talking with Christine, she admitted that she probably didn't provide her students with clear models of what she expected from them for a reading response. When I looked at the student work, I knew we needed to do some serious backtracking!

The first thing that I did was gather samples of strong reading responses from another fourth-grade classroom. Christine and I then had students read through the responses and asked them to tell us what they noticed about the responses. What made these responses so good? We also discussed with her class that responses to literature were a chance for them to share their thinking about the text. It was through this process of looking at other responses that students identified the elements of a strong response. As a class, we then generated a list of criteria that we wanted in our responses.

Criteria for a Quality Reading Response
- Title of the book
- Restatement of the response question
- Developed thinking reflected in the length of the response
- Personal opinion that is supported with evidence from the text (at least three details)
- A conclusion to wrap it all up

After generating this list, Christine and I then had students go back to their own reading notebooks and select what they would consider one of their best reading responses. Students reread their response and assessed their performance using the newly generated criteria. As Heidi Andrade writes, "If students produce it, they can assess it; and if they can assess it, they can improve it" (2007/2008, 61).

It was ironic that Jacob actually selected the same reading response for *Stink* that Christine had brought to the October new-teacher group meeting (see Figure 7.4). Upon reviewing his response, Jacob noted that it needed a conclusion, a title, and at least three examples to support his thinking on why he thought Stink was feeling bad. Christine and I collected all of the responses with the students' notes on them. We then wrote a comment to each child, identifying a strength that we noticed and pointing out an area that he or she might have explored further in the response. In Jacob's response, I noted that he did have a restatement and let the reader know that he thought that Stink was feeling bad but that he could strengthen his response by using specific evidence from the text that would support this opinion.

We felt it was important that students received feedback throughout the entire reteaching process and that they had opportunities to self-assess their work. "When students use feedback from the teacher to learn how to self-assess and set goals, they increase ownership of their own success. In this type of assessment environment, teachers and students collaborate in an ongoing process using assessment information to improve rather than judge learning" (Chappuis and Chappuis 2007/2008, 17).

Writing Reading Responses: Guided Practice

Once we felt students had a clear understanding of what a reading response should look and sound like, we wanted them to have an opportunity (right away) to write another response with guided support. We let students know that we would be reading the book *Just a Dream* by Chris Van Allsburg (1990) as a class (students also had their own copy of the text) and that they would be writing a response to the following question: What message do you think the author is trying to teach us through the character of Walter? We gave them the question up front to help them set a purpose for the reading. We also gave students the rubric we would be using to assess the responses so that they could also use the rubric as a quick self-assessment tool (see Figure 7.5; blank version in appendix). Even

Figure 7.5

READING RESPONSE RUBRIC

Name: _____

Book Title: *Just a Dream*

Author: Chris Van Allsburg

Question: What message do you think the author is trying to teach us through the character of Walter?

	Does Not Meet	**Partially Meets**	**Meets**
Restatement			
Details from the Text to Support Thinking (at least three)			
Concluding Statement			
Stays on Topic			
Uses Proper Conventions			

before reading the book, we wrote a partial restatement as a class on the board, and Christine and I let students know that this could work as the start of their first sentence of the response.

Partial Restatement:
I think the author is trying to teach us . . .

In addition to supporting them in their restatement, we gave students sticky notes so they could hold their thinking as they found evidence in the text to support their opinion.

After reading the story to the class, we asked students to reread the text independently and write a reading response to the question we had presented. Christine and I also circulated, talking with students about their thinking and their plan of what they were going to write.

Christine and I were thrilled with the student responses. Our investment of two forty-five-minute teaching periods was well worth the payoff (see Figure 7.6). The reading responses from the students communicated an

Figure 7.6

RETEACHING READING RESPONSES: A SUMMARY

Through the process of reteaching literature responses, Christine and I helped students identify the elements found in strong responses. We were then able to create a rubric for students so that they understood what they needed to include in their own responses.

- Students read through several model reading responses.
- As a class, we discussed what we noticed about the responses. What made them so good?
- We generated a class list of criteria for a strong reading response.
- Students chose an old reading response they considered their best. They then reread the response and self-assessed it based on newly generated criteria.
- Students were given the response question ahead of time so that they were able to read with a specific purpose. Response Question: What message do you think the author is trying to teach us through the character of Walter?
- Students were also given an assessment rubric so that they were clear on how their reading response would be assessed.
- We read *Just a Dream* by Chris Van Allsburg to students so that they could write new responses. Students also had their own copies of the text that they could refer to for supporting evidence.
- Students wrote their reading responses based on the book, and then they were assessed and feedback was given to the students.
- Students had an additional opportunity for independent practice writing a reading response using the book *The Wretched Stone* by Chris Van Allsburg.

SAMPLE READING RESPONSES BEFORE AND AFTER RETEACHING

A. Todd's November Reading Response to *Frindle*

Nick Granger is a very talented in the trickery category nothing else. This year he is in fifth grade. Nick knows almost every trick in the book. You think this would be easy right? Wrong he is facing Mrs. Granger. And she knows all about tricks and how to use them. So this will be a hard year.

B. Todd's January Reading Response to *Just a Dream* **After Reteaching**

I think the author is trying to teach us that what goes around comes around. For one thing, when Walter littered he dreamed that the Earth was a wasteland. Another thing he said was that trees were stupid. He then dreamed that a lot of trees were being cut down. My final fact is that he threw his trash away and planted a tree. That night he dreamed he was in a wonderful beautiful place. Those facts support my suggestion.

A. Laura's November Reading Response to *Stink*

I would love to have a super galactic jawbreaker. Stink had a super galactic jawbreaker. He spent a week licking it and it turned his tongue blue and his hand green. He licked it in the morning and on the way home from school. And in the end he bit it and it did not break his jaw. He was mad. He wrote a letter to the people that made the jawbreaker saying that they lied and that it did not break his jaw when he bit it.

B. Laura's January Reading Response to *Just a Dream* **After Reteaching**

I think the author is teaching us not to be lazy. One example was when Walter just dumped all the garbage in one of the cans. The second example was when Walter was done with his jelly donut bag and he threw it on the ground—that's littering. The third example is when Walter just sat there watching the show about the future. Then his dream that night took him to all kinds of places in the future. He saw mountains of trash, cutting down trees, and a smoggy Grand Canyon. Walter learned not to be lazy and to recycle. That is what I think he is trying to teach us—not to be lazy.

Figure 7.7

understanding of the text and reflected the expectations that Christine and I had set forth (see Figure 7.7). Even though Jacob's response was still limited in its development, it clearly articulated a position and was supported with evidence from the text (see Figure 7.8). The other positive was that higher-performing students like Todd and Laura worked to their ability and communicated a deeper level of thinking through their reading responses.

Figure 7.8
Jacob's Reading
Response to
Just a Dream

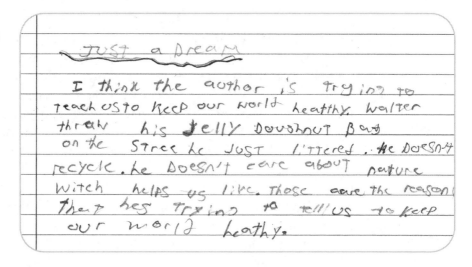

Just a Dream

I think the author 's trying to teach us to keep our world healthy. Walter threw his Jelly Doughnut Bag on the Stree he Just littered. He Doesn't recycle. He Doesn't care about nature witch helps us like. Those are the reason That hes trying to tell us to keep our world heathy.

Independent Practice

After providing feedback to all of the students on their reading response to *Just a Dream*, we then gave them an additional opportunity to write a reading response independently to the picture book *The Wretched Stone* by Chris Van Allsburg (1999). This time students were not supported in their restatement. We simply gave them a response question and rubric and asked them to respond to the text. Having students follow the procedure one more time on their own with a similar text confirmed to Christine and me that they now had a clear understanding of writing reading responses and that they were truly capable of sharing their thinking about books through writing.

After the success of reteaching written response, Christine shared that her student-led book discussions were in a fourth-grade slump and could do with some reenergizing. She asked if we could revisit criteria for elements of strong literature discussions.

It was through the reteaching of reading response that Christine began to see reteaching and assessment as a continuous cycle. It is hard to acknowledge that sometimes you have to "go back" in order to go forward when the emphasis is on covering the curriculum.

Keeping Students at the Heart of Our Conversations

As my children participate in more sports, I find myself at a lot of practices! I have become completely intrigued with how coaches work with their players. I remember the first All-Star practice of last year. Within the first five minutes of practice, I watched Coach Keith Morang give oral feedback and pointers to all nine of the players on the field. He provided immediate feedback to all of the kids. Student performance was at the heart of his formative assessments. I sat on the sidelines in awe of this rapid-fire approach. All of the comments were tailored to the individual needs of the kids. He even went over to a few players and adjusted body positions. As he hit the ball to the catcher, he watched the boy's position and shouted, "Good catch, David, but sit up a little in your stance!" He then hit the ball to my son, Ben. As Ben threw the ball back, Keith responded, "Don't stretch out too early." Keith was able to observe his players this very first practice and move from one to the next, providing feedback that would move them forward individually and as a team.

At the end of that practice, Ben walked off the field with a huge smile and said, "Now that's practice!" I asked, "What made it so good? What makes Keith such a good coach?" Ben responded, "A good coach can get everything out of their players."

I think as teachers we can learn from coaches like Keith, and players like Ben. I believe if good teachers, like good coaches, tailor instruction and provide meaningful feedback, they will get everything out of their students. And if students, like players, are clear on expectations and are involved and invested in the learning process, they too will give all that they can and more!

CHAPTER EIGHT

Curriculum Planning

If one does not know to which port one is sailing,
no wind is favorable.

SENECA

A huge dragon created by the students snaked around the corners of the room; maps and books were sprawled everywhere. As the principal opened the door to the classroom, I glanced around, pleased to see all of the students working comfortably throughout the room on the floor, many in pairs or in groups—all engaged in their independent research inquiries of China. As a new teacher, I was excited to show off the learning that we were doing in our classroom. The principal walked around the room and then simply asked me, "Why are you teaching about China? Where is China in our curriculum?" I paused. To be honest, I wasn't able to articulate why I was teaching China except that I thought it was interesting and that the students seemed eager to learn about faraway places. I knew that it connected to curriculum but was unable to communicate any specifics. All I was able to say was that it made a great topic for an interdisciplinary study. At that stage in my teaching life I couldn't see very far into the future. If I had planned for the following week, I felt that I was in very good shape, and I certainly don't remember being that concerned with curriculum.

Even with specific grade-level district curriculum, it took me nearly ten years to interpret and translate what the curriculum was supposed to look like in my classroom. And chances are my interpretation probably still varied from my colleagues'. One of the differences for new teachers today in regard to curriculum demands compared with when I started teaching is the increased amount of content that needs to be covered coupled with higher levels of accountability for implementing and assessing the curriculum. In supporting new teachers with curriculum planning, we need to not only ensure that they understand state and district standards but, at the same time, help them find room within their year to experiment in the curriculum, encouraging them to bring their own individual strengths and passions into the classroom as I did with my study of China.

Curriculum planning is a challenge for new teachers, like so many other things in their first teaching jobs. This is the first time that they are faced with having to do this type of planning over an extended period of time—the entire school year. Many new teachers struggle just to keep their heads above water, day in and day out, as I did. They are working full time to create and sustain a community of learners, manage classroom behaviors, and wade through curriculum guides in order to try to figure out what they are supposed to teach on a day-to-day basis.

Over the years I have often heard the frustrations of new teachers trying to figure out on a Friday what they were going to teach on a Monday. This type of short-term planning lends itself to filling in school days with isolated activities as opposed to thoughtful strategy instruction. We know this is not efficient or effective for student learning. Robert Marzano, in his book *What Works in Schools: Translating Research into Action*, points out that "a guaranteed and viable curriculum is the school-level factor with the most impact on student achievement" (2003, 22).

It took me years to finally understand the importance of delivering a consistent curriculum and to recognize the impact it had on students' learning—and to appreciate that it was equally important to be able to communicate to others (administrators, teachers, parents, and students) what I was teaching and why. In looking back on my China unit, I don't think there was anything wrong with what I was teaching, but what was lacking was that I couldn't immediately articulate how it connected to the skills and content in the curriculum.

I remember many years ago, when I first started working as a literacy coach, asking a fifth-grade teacher where she was headed in her plans. The teacher responded, "I have this great lesson on apples that I got from a friend of mine." The whole time she was talking, I was thinking, Where does that fit into our curriculum? Another aha moment, as I found myself thinking that very same question my principal had asked me about my China unit so many years ago.

I believe one of our jobs as literacy coaches is to lift new teachers out of the "day-to-day, moment-to-moment" mentality with curriculum planning. We also need to help them see, understand, and master the curriculum expectations in the school and district and to support teachers of any age or experience level to talk in terms of skills and strategies that are being learned through any lesson or unit.

Supporting New Teachers in Curriculum Planning

In an effort to support new teachers with curriculum planning, Leslie and I build time into our monthly new-teacher group meetings to explore, make sense of, and plan out district curriculum. New teachers engage in long-range planning (the big picture of the units and genres that need to be taught over the course of the year) and short-range planning (month-to-month planning of what they are going to teach next). We find that teachers benefit from the scaffold of month-to-month planning and check-in because it's easy to miss some of the long-range plans and needs if you don't have regular times in which you stop, reflect, and look at the year as a whole.

Curriculum Planning Resources

Every classroom teacher has a grade-specific literacy notebook. It is a core literacy resource for all teachers in the district and holds mandated curriculum, assessment information, instructional strategies, and anchor papers for common grade-level assessments. We use these notebooks as a resource in the planning process with new teachers.

Contents of the Literacy Notebook
- Fall/Spring Grade-Specific Literacy Expectations
- ELA Curriculum
- Grade-Specific Common Assessments
- District Core Assessment Tools
  —Developmental Reading Assessment
  —District Writing Prompt
  —Elementary Spelling Inventory
- End-of-Year Filing Directions for Assessments in Student Cumulative Folders

The notebook outlines the literacy expectations for each grade level and also helps to ensure consistency in curricular and assessment expectations. New teachers refer to this information throughout the planning process.

In working with new teachers to plan out curriculum, we keep several questions in mind:

- How do we best support new teachers so that they can wrap their heads around district curriculum and state standards?
- What resources are available to new teachers to help them figure out grade-level expectations?
- How might we guide or redirect a teacher who looks at curriculum as something he or she just needs to "cover" as opposed to material that students need to learn?
- Are there opportunities for grade-level teachers to share how they deliver curriculum over the course of the year?
- How can the new teachers' mentors support them in looking at and planning out curriculum?
- How do we continue to use student work to inform and to guide our planning?
- How do we guide new teachers when they tell us they can't fit it all in?

Our hope is that new teachers embrace curriculum planning as a continuous process—one that is revisited every year, and one that reflects the current needs of their students.

Long-Range Planning: Charting the Course

Early in the year we ask new teachers to sketch out an overview of the upcoming year. We want them to have a long-range plan and overview of the topics and concepts that are to be covered during the year. The teachers start this process in the group, working alongside one another as they sort through curriculum and plot out tentative plans. Leslie and I are also there during this planning time to walk them through the process.

The teachers' mentors and content-area curriculum leaders, who are full-time classroom teachers, also play a huge role in curriculum planning. They walk teachers through the planning of content areas other than literacy. Christine as a first-year teacher received planning support from her mentor for social studies, the science curriculum leader for her science units, and the math coach for the core math program.

The new teachers have ongoing opportunities during monthly team meetings to share their thinking and talk about curriculum plans with their mentors and other grade-level teachers. These grade-level team meetings are focused on curriculum and are a chance for new teachers to find out how their peers fit that curriculum into the school year; the meetings also give veteran teachers a fresh interpretation on how grade-level curriculum can be implemented. We want new and veteran teachers communicating with one another to ensure a common interpretation and understanding of the curriculum within the grade level and across the district.

Leslie and I have created several templates for curriculum planning. We have shifted from paper templates to electronic ones. New teachers use the templates to plot out their overview. Leslie and I initiate this process. At the beginning of the year, Leslie models plotting out her own curriculum chart and shares her thinking behind her decisions. The teachers are able to see from the start that this is a continuous process, one that continues beyond the first few years of teaching. Leslie continues to model the process throughout the year on her own templates. Teachers revisit their overview each month and go back and adjust and record what units were actually taught. New teachers tend to be overly optimistic about what's feasible to teach and tend to plan on covering more than they actually manage to do. We find that the teachers in their first year of induction tend to focus on simply plotting out the units of curriculum and that it is during their second and third year of teaching that they start to tease out their plans and become more purposeful in their alignment and placement of curriculum across the year. It is through their actual teaching experiences that they gain a better sense of what works and what doesn't.

In looking at Christine's template (Figure 8.1 shows a draft from midyear), I noticed that it reflects mostly mandated curriculum. However, it was right around this time that she stuck in a couple of units of her own choice that she wanted to try out—poetry and an author study on Chris Van Allsburg. Her added units still connected to key content and skills that needed to be covered within the curriculum, but she personalized the avenue in which to present those skills—maintaining her sense of individuality.

One of the ways I supported Christine her first year was by gently nudging her to articulate the skills and content taught through various literature books and starting to model how to line them up with curriculum. Christine was confident in selecting books that would meet the range of needs in her classroom, and she was diligent about recording their titles in her monthly planning (see Figure 8.2). But when I asked her what her focus was with the books, she was not as confident in articulating why those

CHRISTINE'S YEAR AT A GLANCE

	Reading	Writing	Word Study	Math	Science	Social Studies	Assessments
September	Whole group Stink series books Setting expectations Graphic organizers Revisit comprehension Strategies Reading with purpose	Memoir writing Revision strategies Launch writing workshop	Sort 1 & 2 Open & closed syllables & junctures	Unit 1 Median graphs	Classification Rocks & minerals	Geography	• Developmental Reading Assessment (DRA) • District Writing Prompt • Elementary Spelling Inventory
October *Move this to spring?	Author Study Andrew Clements Launching literature discussions Strategies to hold thinking	Finish memoir Choice	Sort 3 & 4 Long vowels in accented syllables	Unit 2 Area Perimeter	Crystals Rock cycle	Mapping	
November	Reading workshop Literature groups Focus on characters Inference	Persuasive turkey letter	Sort 5 & 6 Vowel pairs ai, ee, ea & oi, oy, ou, ow	Unit 3 Subtraction	Fossils	Mapping (continents) Election	
December	Reading workshop Informational texts Biographies	Multigenre choice	Sort 7 & 8 Vowels au, aw, al & r- influenced a	Unit 4 Multiply	Fossils	Maine	

continued

Figure 8.1

Month	Reading	Writing	Word Study	Math	Science	Social Studies	Assessment
January	Reading workshop / Literature groups / Story structure / Elements of biographies / Determining important information	Choice (character; BME) / Autobiography	Sort 9 & 10 / r- influenced o & w before vowels	Units 5, 6, 7 / Best fit lines estimate / Bouncy ball / Place values	Energy (Light)	Maine cont.	
February	Reading workshop / Literature groups / Theme	Finish autobiographies	Sort 11 & 12 / er/ sound: er, ir, ur, er, ear, ere, eer & r- influenced e	Unit 7 cont.	Energy (Sound)	Government	
March *Next year move reading response focus to October	MEA TESTING 2 WEEKS / Revisit reading responses / Author study (whole group) Chris Van Allsburg / Synthesis	Research: Search Is On	Sort 13 & 14 / final syllable -le, -el, -il, al		Energy (Heat = optional) / Inventions & Inventors cards	States	• Search Is On (Grade-level assessment) • Maine Educational Assessments (State testing)
April	Student choice / Book clubs (fiction and nonfiction)	Independent research	Sort 15 & 16 / final syllable -er, -ar, -or & agents/ comparatives		Life cycle / Living things	D.C.	
May	Poetry?	Poetry?	Sort 17 & 18 / er/ sound: -cher, -ture, -sure, -ure & /en/ sound: -en, -on, -an, -ain		Oceans (Adopt an animal?)	Mexico	
June			Sort 19 & 20 / initial syllables a-, de-, be- & hard/ soft c & g		Oceans	Canada	• Developmental Reading Assessment (DRA) • District Writing Prompt • Elementary Spelling Inventory

Figure 8.1 (continued)

Christine's Two-Month Curriculum Plan

	Reading	Writing	Math	Science	Social Studies	Assessments
November	**Read Aloud:** Lost on a Mountain in Maine (Donn Fendler) **Literature Group Books:** 1. Doing Time Online (Jan Siebold) 2. My Father's Dragon (Ruth Stiles Gannett) 3. The Fear Place (Phyllis Reynolds Naylor) **Comprehension Focus:** Inference *Focus on Characters **Word Study:** Sort 5 & 6 Vowel pairs ai, ee, ea & oi, oy, ou, ow **Fluency:** Phrasing and expression	**Genre:** Multigenre (snapshot, narrative, poem, letter, interview, comic, third person) **Craft Focus:** Persuasion Point of view (turkey letters) Multigenre: Snapshots **Conventions/Mechanics Focus:** Beginning/end punctuation	**Focus Topic:** Unit 3 Numbers and Operations	Fossils	Maine Election	
December	**Read Aloud:** Fantastic Mr. Fox (Roald Dahl) **Literature Group Books:** Time for Kids Biography Series 1. Eleanor Roosevelt: First Lady of the World (Dina El Nabli) 2. Jackie Robinson: Strong Inside and Out (Denise Lewis Patrick) 3. Harriet Tubman: A Woman of Courage (Renee Skelton) 4. Benjamin Franklin: A Man of Many Talents (Kathryn Satterfield) *Focus on Elements of Biography Genre and Character Traits **Comprehension Focus:** Determining important information **Word Study:** Sort 7 & 8 Vowels au, aw, al & r-influenced **Fluency:** Poetry for phrasing	**Genre:** Continue Multigenre **Craft Focus:** Alternative leads **Conventions/Mechanics Focus:** Dialogue as craft	**Focus Topic:** Unit 4 Factors and Products	Fossils Energy	Government Continue Maine Studies	

Figure 8.2

books were selected and the literary concepts taught through them. Early in November I sat with her looking at the district's curriculum and pointed out that the books that she had chosen would lend themselves to focusing in on character and showed her the curriculum indicators that addressed character development. At that point, she went back into the template and added the focus on character with the intention of using that idea next year. We then looked ahead at what she was planning for December. I noticed Christine had written down that she would teach biographies in December and identified specific book ideas but again wasn't specific in what aspect of the curriculum was being addressed through the biography unit. As before, we looked at the curriculum guide and targeted specific curriculum. In the end she decided to focus on teaching elements of biographies and work with students on determining important information, laying the foundation for a future writing/research unit on biographies. Part of the process is helping teachers see the connections between instruction and curriculum and extend those connections across content areas.

At times, teachers have found that they didn't like where they placed a particular unit. This past year Christine placed her author study of Andrew Clements early in the year; however, in reflecting on the unit, she decided that for next year she would like to place it later in the year. She recorded when she had taught the author study but made a note to herself that she needed to rethink the placement of the unit for the following year. Realistically, it often takes new teachers the whole year just to sketch an overview of it.

We find that teachers start to sprinkle more individuality and passion into their planning once they have a solid grasp of the district curriculum. Once teachers have cracked how to incorporate the skills and strategies the curriculum calls for into the content they want to teach, they feel more confident to develop their own units of study, satisfying both the district and themselves. For example, in Jessica's third year of teaching, she developed an interdisciplinary unit on mystery. As she developed the unit, she was specific and purposeful in outlining the skills and content from the curriculum that she was covering through the unit—she knew what she was teaching and why and was excited to add this new piece to her year.

Short-Range Planning: Looking Ahead a Month at a Time

We also encourage new teachers to sketch out a more detailed overview of monthly plans. We have provided a skeletal template that they can use for this but encourage them to find an organizational system that works for them.

We want teachers to really look ahead and think about genre studies for writing and literature books that they might use for guided reading groups. Christine's notes are brief and are intended to guide her in her more specific weekly plans (see Figure 8.2).

On the other hand, Katie, a newer third-grade teacher, likes space to create more detailed plans. She took the concept of the template and designed her own organizational system by making individual templates for each month. This allowed her to write more detailed monthly overviews (see Figure 8.3). Katie shared at one of our meetings: "I was so excited after our last meeting that I went home and worked on my plans

Figure 8.3

KATIE'S MONTHLY OVERVIEW PLANS

September

Notes: Work on building a community, building reading stamina.

Assessments & Events
- DRA
- Writing Prompt
- Spelling Inventory
- EMT

Reading
Feature Author: Kevin Henkes
Read-Aloud: *The Mouse and the Motorcycle*
Literature Books: ~
Comprehension Focus: Previewing texts, making predictions, character traits
Vocabulary Words:
Other: Introduce reading responses, copy, guess, check, character-traits
    graphic organizer

Writing
Genre: Poetry
Craft Focus:
Conventions/Mechanics Focus:

Word Study
Sorts: Long-vowel patterns

Math
Units: 1 & 2

Theme
Units & Objectives: Community Building
Mapping:

for hours, going all the way back to the beginning of the school year. I even blew off my graduate work—that speaks volumes! Having this plotted out gives me a sense of where I am and where I am headed. These plans will be so helpful in planning, especially next year."

Jessica still prefers doing her curriculum planning with paper and pencil on the same old planning templates that she used in her first year of teaching. When I asked Jessica about the method that she has embraced for planning, she said, "I still use the old templates you gave me my first year of teaching. I am constantly revisiting them. My planning is always in process; the templates are constantly changing and full of smudged eraser marks, but they really do serve as my home base for planning."

What Does Planning Time Look Like?

Planning time is scheduled into every monthly new-teacher group meeting. It is the one item that never gets moved off the agenda and is a time designated for new teachers to use as needed for planning purposes. They are accountable to themselves. Although their plans are never turned in to anyone, Leslie and I do conference individually with them to get a sense of where they are in their planning, and administrators will reference the planning templates during individual conferences with the teachers.

During the curriculum planning time of our group meetings, there is usually a busy hum in the room. Laptops and planning templates are pulled out while teachers talk with one another and share ideas. Teachers also use this time to go and browse through the book closets to select new books for the upcoming months. It is a time to gather resources. Leslie and I work with them as they gather those resources, select books for their reading workshop, and write out their yearly and monthly plans.

Reflecting on What Was Taught Versus What Was Planned

The monthly plans serve as a detailed record of what teachers have taught each month and a projection of where they are going. It is not enough to just write out plans. Each month we encourage the teachers to analyze student work, look at their templates, and reflect on what was actually taught and learned as they move ahead to the upcoming month and plot out projected ideas. We all know that we may have the best intentions for moving through a unit and find that it either takes us longer than planned or that the students just didn't get it.

An example of this was when Christine and I revisited reading responses with her students as a result of looking at their work (see Chapter 7). We made the decision to go back and reteach reading responses to her class as a whole group. This change in plans interrupted projected plans, and adjustments needed to be made.

Why Curriculum Planning?

New teachers should not go through their first few years feeling that they don't have a plan and that they are on an unknown journey. It's not good for the teachers. It's not good for the students.

As a new teacher, my own insecurity about what to teach and my superficial understanding of our district curriculum was reflected in my limited repertoire of routes to and from school: just one, in fact—straight up the highway to the Waterville exit. During one of the first snowstorms of the season, I was on the interstate driving home only to be rerouted off an unfamiliar exit. I had no idea where I was; it seemed to me that I was in the middle of nowhere in the midst of a snowstorm. This was before everyone had cell phones and GPS in their cars. I remember driving off the highway in disbelief, wondering how this could be happening to me. I stopped at the stop sign as I exited the ramp thinking, Should I go left or should I go right? I had absolutely no idea how to get home. I didn't know where I was, or in which direction I should head. The feeling of not knowing was unsettling. This moment captured how I was feeling as a new teacher. I was tired of not knowing, and tired of just getting by. As I sat at the exit not knowing which way to turn, I saw a moving truck with *Augusta, Maine*, lettered on its side just a few cars ahead of me. I decided to follow it. But the whole time I followed it on those snowy roads, I questioned whether I had made the correct decision. It was the strangest feeling driving and not really knowing if I was headed in the right direction—much like my planning of curriculum at the time.

I knew my destination was Augusta, Maine, but at the time I had no flexibility or tools to steer off the path or get to my destination in another way. My original route home took me just one way, and did not account for any variables.

By contrast, Jessica's experience as a first-year teacher was very different. Jess was positive, upbeat, and always seemed to know where she was headed next in the classroom. However, her experience reflects having had ongoing support in the area of curriculum planning through new-teacher induction. Jess often shared that having time to plan was one of the greatest benefits of meeting together as a group each month. In one of her early journal entries as a new teacher, she wrote: "Our meetings greatly affect my planning. I have the map of the big picture to refer to and know what is expected in the curriculum. I love that feeling of knowing what I am supposed to do and the flexibility to modify and refine it based on the needs of my students."

We want to support new teachers, like Jessica, in the planning process right from the start. We want them to know the road map of curricular expectations in the district and give them tools so that they can have the flexibility to move in different ways as they learn from students and reflect upon what has worked and what hasn't worked in their plans. It is our hope that these curriculum plans serve as their "home base," a point of reference that helps maintain their direction amid all storminess; a plan that guides them as they drive onward in their instructional journey.

CHAPTER NINE

Study Groups: Where New and Veteran Teachers Learn Together

We believe professional learning communities are an excellent way to provide the support, collegiality, intellectual stimulation, and feedback for our less experienced teachers. The connectedness that grows out of studying, learning, and finding new ways to be effective will provide meaning for themselves personally and make a difference professionally.

SHIRLEY HORDE AND WILLIAM SOMMERS, 2008

One of my favorite inventions ever is the self-cleaning oven. Set a timer, lock the oven door, and a few hours later—voila! You have a clean oven and can feel virtuous about it, even though it required almost no effort on your part.

For nearly twenty years I have worked with Brenda Power, editor of *Choice Literacy*. Together we have spent hours discussing what we feel are the key organizational elements that lend themselves to effective professional study groups. About a year ago, Brenda pointed out to me that study groups are like self-cleaning ovens—put a few key elements in place, and they can almost run themselves. I have to admit I wanted to believe that I had more to do with the success of our study groups than just a predictable schedule and a few key components! But the more I have thought about it, the more I've come to believe that Brenda is right—study groups really are like self-cleaning ovens that can run virtually on their own.

I wrote extensively about study groups in my last book, *Becoming a Literacy Leader: Supporting Learning and Change* (2006). I feel strongly that study groups are an essential component to new-teacher induction, and in this chapter I will focus on the benefits they can offer new teachers. These include:

- Membership in a professional learning community
- The opportunity to learn alongside veteran colleagues
- A built-in support system
- A sense of collegiality
- Self-directed learning
- Sustained professional development

Harry Wong believes that "what keeps good teachers are structured, sustained, intensive professional development programs that allow new teachers to observe others, to be observed by others and to be part of networks or study groups where all teachers share together, grow together, and learn to respect other's work" (2005, 46). Study groups are a vehicle for new teachers to share their point of view with other colleagues in a comfortable and nonthreatening environment.

Study groups are all about choice. They are the one professional development opportunity that new teachers can choose to join or not to join. Study groups present new teachers with the chance to select a topic of interest and participate in authentic learning communities with their teaching peers. As Shirley Horde and William Sommers write in reference to less experienced teachers, "The connectedness that grows out of studying, learning, and finding new ways to be effective will provide meaning for themselves personally and make a difference professionally" (2008, 150). Jessica wrote the following testimonial to the value of study groups after her first year of teaching: "I like participating in study groups because they give me a chance to connect with colleagues who have similar interests as me. Our busy days limit our professional development discussions, but study groups allow us to share new thinking and successful lesson plans or activities and to learn from each other."

The Nuts and Bolts of Study Groups

We used to spend hours looking for the perfect activity or icebreaker for groups, but over time we've found that a standard format with regular components works best for us. Teachers who come to the group know what to expect. It's not that they aren't exposed to new things, but it's all within a structure that invites comfort and reflection, key elements for incorporating new teachers into these inquiry groups. Here are the components of our study groups that help to provide consistency and make it seem as though they are running themselves:

- One-hour time frame
- Discussion time at the start
- Video viewing
- Reading time
- Whole-group discussion

One-Hour Time Frame

We've tried longer and shorter formats, and one hour is just right for not requiring too much of a commitment from teachers, while still allowing for in-depth exploration of a topic. We provide the schedule months in advance, so that everyone can plan appointments and activities around the study-group meeting.

Discussion Time at the Start

We like to focus the group at the start of the meeting with a couple of questions related to the topic, or just by discussing what everyone has tried related to the theme since the last meeting. This is a transition time—we can sense everyone relaxing and switching gears from place to place.

Video Viewing

We've found that many teachers will not read professional books. We can lament over all the reasons why these teachers don't enjoy professional reading, but the point is we can't be certain teachers will read books we give them outside of the study groups. For this reason, we always include short video snippets so that we have a shared experience with professional best practice. In addition to videos, we have started to incorporate podcasts into our groups. Podcasts are a no-cost option to hear interviews firsthand with some of our favorite authors.

We've found it's important to watch no more than a five- to ten-minute segment of a video during a study group—there is so much going on in each minute of a classroom video that more than a few minutes is overload in a professional setting. We watch one lesson, or one conference with a student, and focus the viewing with a note-taking task. For example, if the video was of a lesson, we might have participants keep two-column notes, with one column labeled What I Notice and the other labeled What I Might Try in My Classroom. (See Two-Column Notes Form in the appendix.)

We use videos and podcasts from Choice Literacy, Stenhouse Publishers, Heinemann, and the Annenberg Foundation—all excellent sources for professional video and interviews featuring authentic classroom examples of reading and writing workshops. (See Study-Group Resources in the appendix.)

Reading Time

Because many teachers are hesitant about reading professional books, we've found that providing reading time during study groups is essential. We either photocopy a brief article or a short excerpt from a book, or highlight a few pages within the book we've purchased for the group to read throughout the year and include five to ten minutes of silent reading time. Even participants who have read the excerpt previously appreciate the time to dig in and reread and have a chance to discuss the reading with their colleagues while it is still fresh.

Whole-Group Discussion

We always close the study group with a whole-group discussion of what was learned and what participants plan to try out in their classrooms before the next session. We also make plans for the next session with the group. For example, if we are working our way through a book together, we talk about reading for the next meeting. We also discuss what video segment we might view, based on what worked and what didn't with that day's video. Participants are welcome to stay after the group and chat, but those on tight family schedules need to know that we will run a tight ship and end each study group on time.

My Role

The group depends on me to know the resource base. If a topic comes up that isn't addressed in the book or article that the group is reading (or is better addressed in another book or article), I'll offer to bring a source that does address the topic to the next session. I always preview the entire video series, so I can make suggestions about what selections might best address the interests emerging in the group. However, my role is limited. I usually sit back during the group and let others to the talking—everyone knows that he or she will have a comfortable place to share classroom triumphs and struggles, so many participants quickly learn to bring a funny story, an inspiring student sample, or a baffling dilemma to share with the group.

Tips for Leading Study Groups

I have led study groups in my own school for the past eight years. Here is the advice I wish that someone had given me when I began my first group:

- Choose a clear focus in advance.
- Seek volunteers—never have mandatory attendance.
- Limit the number of participants. (I've found eight or fewer works well.)
- Set meeting dates in advance so participants can reserve them.
- Order books for everyone in advance.
- Organize resources for participants.
- Limit sessions to an hour, and stick to the time limit.
- Meet in a relaxed, comfortable environment.
- Provide plenty of refreshments.
- Don't teach—the goal is a conversation where everyone talks freely.
- Establish a predictable format.

For more general background on book clubs for adults and advice on thorny issues like how to deal with participants who dominate discussions, visit the Reading Group Guides clearinghouse at http://www .readinggroupguides.com/. Free study guides that contain discussion points and activities to specific Stenhouse titles can be downloaded at http://www.stenhouse.com/html/pdguides.htm.

Incorporating Cofacilitators

As our groups have evolved, teachers have taken more of a leadership role in the implementation and facilitation of those groups. This year I even incorporated cofacilitators. Every study group had a teacher cofacilitator, a practice that I will continue to implement next year since it empowers the group. Although I do much of the behind-the-scenes work of sifting through resources and preparing agendas, the actual group is led by the cofacilitating teacher. Although the leadership is evolving to include all teachers, participants still expect the routines of video viewing, reading, and discussion each week, moving easily between jotting notes and chatting.

With these elements in place, our study groups look remarkably similar from group to group, though the content and the group dynamics vary greatly.

Menu of Study Groups

The first step in setting up the study groups is creating a menu of groups for the teachers to select from (see Figure 9.1). I start thinking about resources for next year's study groups halfway through the school year. You may be wondering how I could possibly be thinking of study groups when I've barely made it through second quarter. I agree that it is too early to set up study groups for the upcoming year, but it is never too early to be scoping out and sifting through the latest resources. My menu is drafted and redrafted throughout the spring as I talk with teachers, meet with study groups, and continue sifting through resources.

Selecting Resources

I am often asked how I select resources for study groups. Resources tend to find their way to me. I find myself jotting down titles that I have either seen in professional catalogs or read online or that have been recommended to me by trusted friends. I look for topics that will be of interest to both new and veteran teachers.

Texts are not randomly selected, nor are they chosen solely because they are newly published. Many of the resources that I offer to teachers are extensions of past study-group topics, deal with concepts that align with school/district initiatives, or help put the literacy pieces together and will appeal to both new and veteran teachers who are continuing to refine their reading and writing workshop.

For example, over the last nine years, I have worked with study-group members to refine their reading workshops. We have read *Beyond Leveled Books* (2001) and *Still Learning to Read* (2003) and have viewed the videotapes *Bringing Reading to Life* (2004) by Franki Sibberson and Karen

SAMPLE STUDY-GROUP OFFERINGS

Assessment in the Reading Workshop

Grades 3–5 (Hall School—Thursday Afternoon Meetings, 3:00)

This group will continue to explore the topic of assessment within reading workshop. We will work with the book *Day-to-Day Assessment in the Reading Workshop: Making Informed Instructional Decisions in Grades 3–6* by Franki Sibberson and Karen Szymusiak (2008). We will layer on assessment video through Choice Literacy Web site.

Notebook Connections: Strategies for the Reader's Notebook

Grades 3–5 (Hall School—Thursday Afternoon Meetings, 3:00, Meet Monthly, October–April)

This group will explore Aimee Buckner's new book. If you loved *Notebook Know-How* (2005) and how Aimee used writer's notebooks with her students, I think you'll also enjoy her new book that focuses in on reading workshop. In *Notebook Connections* (2009), Aimee leads readers through the process of launching, developing, and fine-tuning reader's notebooks.

Graphica

Grades 3–5 (Hall School—Thursday Afternoon Meetings, 3:00, Meet Monthly, October–April)

This group will read Terry Thompson's book *Adventures in Graphica: Using Comics and Graphic Novels to Teach Comprehension, 2–6* (2008). We will explore how graphic texts can be used to create a bridge as students transfer abstract comprehension strategies learned through comics and graphic novels to traditional texts.

What's New in Children's Literature?

Grades 3–5 (Hall School—Monday Morning Meetings, 7:15, Meet Monthly, October–April)

This one is back by request again for another year! We will explore a new children's book each month and also look at a few popular book blogs that will serve as resources to find new and engaging books for our students. Participants rotate selecting the new book of the month for the group.

Book Discussion: *Keeping Katherine*

Grades 3–5 (Hall School—One-Shot Literature Discussion in Fall)

This group will read *Keeping Katherine: A Mother's Journey to Acceptance*, a memoir by Susan Zimmermann (2004). Susan tells the story of life with her daughter Katherine—a child who developed normally until she was a year old and then stopped developing, becoming severely handicapped by age two. Katherine was later diagnosed with Rett syndrome.

Designing Learning Environments

Grades 3–5 (A Two-Hour Session the Week Before School, 9:00–11:00)

This will be the third consecutive year of offering this group. It will again be a two-hour, *one-shot* session held one morning the week before school starts followed up with one meeting in the spring. In this group we will ask ourselves if our room design reflects our educational beliefs about learning. We will also share last-minute ideas for classroom design. We will watch clips from the DVD *Simply Organized: Classroom Libraries and Storage Areas* (2008) by Gail Boushey and Joan Moser ("The Sisters"). We will explore Debbie Miller's new book, *Teaching with Intention: Defining Beliefs, Aligning Practice, Taking Action, K–5* (2008).

Figure 9.1

Szymusiak. Nine years later we are continuing to refine our reading workshop, but with more of an emphasis on formative assessment. It made sense to include Franki and Karen's new book, *Day-to Day-Assessment in the Reading Workshop: Making Informed Instructional Decisions in Grades 3–6* (2008) as a new study-group offering. Another text selection that we've included is the memoir *Keeping Katherine: A Mother's Journey to Acceptance* by Susan Zimmermann (2004). This is not a professional literacy text. Over the last few years, however, we have moved away from working with only professional texts to support our learning. We have started reading memoirs. We have found them to be a way for us to reflect on our own process as readers and that they offer us an authentic opportunity for an adult literature discussion. Memoirs also provide a lens to study writer's craft through an author's writing. Our staff text last year was *The Glass Castle* by Jeannette Walls (2005), and we had a study group reading Stephen King's memoir, *On Writing* (2000). In putting together the study-group offerings, I was thinking that some staff would want to continue exploring memoirs as a vehicle for their literacy learning.

During the spring I continue to collect and share resources with staff. I ask for their input and gauge interest levels before putting out an official offering of study groups for the upcoming year. I also send out an e-mail asking for teacher volunteers who would be interested in cofacilitating a study group with me. My list of offerings is always revised from the draft version. Topics and resources that are interesting to me may not grab the interest of the teachers I work with, or they might suggest other books or videos within a theme to consider.

Taking a Closer Look at a Study Group

This past year one of our study groups read the book *Boy Writers: Reclaiming Their Voices* by Ralph Fletcher (2006) (see Figure 9.2). We found through our discussions that we all held strong opinions around boys, writing, and technology. This particular study group is where I noticed our increased confidence and willingness to challenge ideas in the book, as well as in our own teaching.

Our study groups have always been a mix of new and veteran teachers. New teachers are being inducted into a school culture that reflects open dialogue and inquiry around focused topics. Staff have been participating in study groups for the last nine years and are comfortable with the learning format that these groups offer and eager to integrate new staff

Figure 9.2

BOY WRITERS STUDY GROUP AGENDA

Discussion (10 minutes)

- Look at your classroom through the eyes of your boys. What is and isn't working for them in your writing classroom?
- Any thoughts from Chapters 1 and 2?

Video Excerpt (15 minutes)

- View video segment of *The Boys Lunch Writing Group* ("Dude, Listen to This!" by Ralph Fletcher).
- Two-column notes: What do you notice? / What do you wonder?
- Group discussion

Reading Excerpt (15 minutes)

- Reread pages 32–36.
- Share your thoughts surrounding the use of instant messaging in the classroom.

Listen to Interview Excerpt (15 minutes)

- Interview: NPR with Ralph Fletcher and Tom Newkirk
  Link: http://nhpr.org/archive/2007/6/21
- Ralph argues that we must widen the circle and give boys more choice if we want to engage them as writers. React to this statement.

Putting Ideas into Practice (5 minutes)

- What might you try? What are you thinking?

into the learning community. As a group, we engage in open and honest discussions, conversations where we respect one another's ideas and point of view but do not necessarily agree. We have become critical thinkers and evaluators of what we read, and not merely a sponge for new ideas. I think in the past we tended to stay silent if we did not agree with one another's thinking. Too often we trusted the information found in new professional books and were quick to doubt ourselves and our instructional methods.

This past year, when we came to the section in *Boy Writers* where Ralph Fletcher addressed instant messaging, we found ourselves in a heated debate about whether or not instant messaging was a tool for our students to become more proficient writers. Many teachers questioned if instant messaging really fostered developed writing. Teachers pulled quotes from the book; others added stories from personal experience (the parents of teens knew what *POS* meant—*parents over shoulder*, a code to let the recipient know the texter was being watched). We had newer (and, yes, younger) teachers like Jessica, who were adept at instant messaging, adding firsthand accounts of how technology was changing their personal literacy and their relationships with peers. Jessica openly embraced technology as a tool that she incorporated as part of her instruction. Instant messaging was part of her life. She realized at that meeting just how little some of us knew about the language of instant messaging. Being the kind, subtle leader that she is, she attempted to bring us up to speed and slipped a copy of "Top 50 Most Commonly Used Text Messaging Terms" into our mailboxes after our meeting. These can be accessed at the following site: http://www.sync-blog.com/sync/2007/12/top-50-most-com.html.

Changing Minds and Changing Classrooms

Instant messaging (IM) was an area where generational differences in our group and different life experiences led to divergent views, especially when it came to the place of this type of communication in classrooms. Many of us went and did further research on instant messaging and found articles that both defended and negated it as an instructional tool.

Maxine, one of our veteran teachers, brought some of those research articles on instant messaging to the group. One of them, "Tapping Instant Messaging" from *Education Week's Digital Directions* (Martineau 2007), noted that IM can be a tool for brainstorming ideas for writing and also highlighted how it could be used for book discussions among students.

Maxine was interested in using instant messaging as a literacy tool within her classroom. She was intrigued by the conversation of the younger teachers like Jessica in the study group and the ease with which they conversed about technology and the role it played in their classrooms. Maxine took on the personal challenge of looking at how she could integrate instant messaging within her classroom. She had the tech team "unlock" the network so that her students could instant message. Instead of just talking about it, she had her students engage in it. This is exactly what we want to happen during study groups—veteran and novice teachers working together and learning from one another.

Maxine brought the transcripts of her fifth graders' instant messaging to one of our study groups. She shared that her first attempt of playing with instant messaging in the classroom with students was really just open conversation. In reflecting on the transcripts, Maxine immediately zoomed in on one of her students, Douglas. It wasn't that this boy said anything profound; rather, it was the fact that he was actually engaged and conversed with his peers through the IM session. This particular student rarely speaks at all in class. Maxine couldn't help but wonder if instant messaging was a key to helping this student become more included within the classroom community.

Example of Douglas (D) participating in the first student IM exchange:
  D: I love elmo!
  M: nancy
  D: do you?
  K: i just washed my hair
  N: lol and Michael Jackson
  M: you look pretty nancy (N)
  N: ok
  D: nancy!
  M: haha
  K: washed my hair thurely
  D: stop
  N: hahhhhhhha
  M: lol
  D: Elmo Rocks!

Maxine continued experimenting with instant messaging and incorporated it into some virtual literature discussions (ironically, she used it as a tool for discussing the book *Fig Pudding*, written by Ralph Fletcher). She also played around with using instant messaging as a brainstorming tool for writing. She wondered if it could serve as a vehicle for freewriting and that maybe instant messaging wasn't about producing developed writing or deep conversations but rather a tool that could help students unleash their thinking. Peter Elbow refers to freewriting as one of the most effective ways to improve writing. The idea is that you just write, without stopping. He believes that "the main thing about freewriting is that it is the *nonediting*. It is an exercise in bringing together the process of producing words and putting them down on the page. Practiced regularly, it undoes the ingrained habit of editing at the same time you are trying to produce. It will make writing less blocked because words will come more easily" (1973, 6). Maxine wondered if instant messaging could have the same freeing power. She continued experimenting with instant messaging in the classroom throughout the year. Instant messaging turned into a personal teacher inquiry project for Maxine. The study group provided her with the continued opportunity to voice her learning.

It was through our study-group meetings on boy writers that Maxine inspired the newer teachers with her strong literacy knowledge and her skills of integrating new ideas with existing literacy practices (IM virtual literature discussions versus student-led discussions and IM for brainstorming writing ideas). And it was new teachers like Jessica who brought a fresh perspective and confidence to the group. In Jessica's case, it was her use of technology in her classroom (Web pages for research, digital storytelling projects, and classroom blogs) that nudged the rest of us to be more open-minded in how it could be used as a tool in our own literacy classrooms.

The level of professional dialogue that occurred during the Boy Writers group is what we strive for in all of our study groups—conversations that revolve around research and student work, ultimately leading us to rethink our practice. A win-win learning environment for all, new and veteran teachers alike.

The Continued Success of Study Groups

The last session of a study group each year is like that wonderful moment when we open our oven and wonder how it miraculously got so clean. We marvel at all we've accomplished in our group during the year. But, while the self-cleaning oven may remain a bit of a mystery to us, we know the success of study groups is due to our belief that we need to let the community evolve over time. If the predictable format and thought-provoking resources are provided, then the learning that takes place over the year always exceeds our expectations and those of the participants.

Final Words: I Believe

I dwell in possibility.

EMILY DICKINSON, 1862 (IN JOHNSON 1976)

I have typically run four to five miles a day since high school. For years I secretly dreamed of doing a marathon, but always stayed within my comfort zone. I longed to run the 26.2 miles and fantasized about crossing the finish line. I figured if Oprah could run a marathon, I could too. A year ago, I started training for one with my neighbor. Together we began to increase our daily and weekly mileage. I was truly excited about this personal challenge but kept this endeavor a secret from friends and family. I didn't tell anyone for fear that I might not be able to meet my goal. I was afraid of failing.

I specifically remember my first nineteen-mile run. It was the first time I hit a running wall! I had blisters and black toenails, not to mention I finished the run barely able to walk. It was the first time during training that I had self-doubt—maybe I wasn't cut out to be a marathoner! It was also the end of summer, and I found myself facing new roadblocks. I was back to working full time, squeezing in morning jogs before work in the dark, and juggling the sports schedules of two kids.

While I was hobbling home after this nineteen-mile run, it hit me that my marathon experience was similar to that of teachers working to implement new instructional practices. I thought of my first year of teaching, so defeated that I didn't think I could go on. I thought of the new teachers I work to support. I wondered what it would take to get me through my first marathon. I wondered what new teachers needed to get through their first few years of teaching.

I believe that my first nineteen-mile run represented what Michael Fullan describes in the educational world as an "implementation dip"— "literally a dip in performance and confidence as one encounters an innovation that requires new skills and new understandings" (2001, 40). As a runner, I was hitting the "bumpiness and difficulties encountered as people learn new behaviors and beliefs."

I thought of new teachers. Everything is new. I know that I entered my first year of teaching with optimism and a contagious enthusiasm for learning. I was ready to execute the new ideas I had experimented with as an undergraduate. But, as so many of the new teachers I work with, I was quickly ready to abandon the classroom by December and fantasized about my next profession (that of a baker) as I hit roadblock after roadblock (lack of materials, inability to manage student behaviors, administering multiple classroom assessments while still trying to teach, juggling pieces of curriculum into the school day).

So what does my running have to do with supporting and retaining new teachers? My running partner was one of my supports. She waited for me at the end of her driveway every morning at 5:00 a.m. She was there slowing down her pace with me on the days that were hard, the days I really didn't want to continue. My children were my personal fan club, telling me without hesitation, "Mom you can do this!" My husband gave me the gift of time to fit in my runs. I believe that my running partner and my family were my collaborative support systems that helped me to overcome the obstacles that I encountered on my way to the marathon.

The New Teacher Center reports that research shows that almost 50 percent of *all* new teachers leave our profession after only five years—and not just those in schools difficult to staff (2006). I believe that collaborative learning environments with on-site support systems are the key to retaining these new teachers in the field of education. I believe that when new teachers are given ongoing opportunities over time to explore new ideas, refine instructional practices, and process thinking among supportive colleagues, they will have the support needed to overcome the roadblocks and challenges they too often face alone as new teachers. I see it as our job as educators to support one another and create learning environments that will nurture and support new teachers.

Teaching is too hard to go about it alone; it is too easy to lose momentum for our new ideas and become discouraged with the profession that at one point we were so excited to join. I believe that built-in layers of support within schools can make a difference in our ability to retain new teachers within districts and our profession.

So what ever happened with my marathon? I finished two marathons last year. I crossed the finish line of the Maine Marathon with my running partner at 3:45, a time that qualified us for the Boston Marathon. We then trained for it through a stormy Maine winter. In Boston, we crossed the finish line together, in step with one another, as our families and thousands of unknown spectators cheered us on.

Training for the marathons taught me firsthand the power support systems can have to help one push through obstacles and obtain goals. I could never have achieved this alone. New teachers depend on our support. I believe it is our job as coaches, teachers, mentors, and administrators—the whole school community—to nurture, encourage, and cheer on new educators as they embark on their journey as teachers, so that they too can cross that finish line.

Appendix

OBSERVATION NOTES FORM

Teacher: _____   Date: _____

Sketch the room on the back.

Focus of Lesson:

Zone in On . . .	Distribution of Time	What Do You Notice?	What Do You Wonder?	What Might You Like to Try?
Teacher (What is the teacher doing?)				
Evidence of Gradual Release				
Student Engagement (What are the students doing?)				
Materials				
Environment				
Assessment (How do you know the students are getting it?)				

Two-Column Notes Form

What I Notice	What I Might Try in My Classroom

Literacy Data Recording Sheet

Teacher:

Grade:

Last Name	First Name	Sp/Ed Speech	ESOL	New Entry	Reading		Writing		Spelling		Research
					Fall	Spring	Fall	Spring	Fall	Spring	Spring

Using Assessments to Inform Instruction

Student	Developmental Reading Assessment (DRA)	Writing Prompt and Writing Sample	Elementary Spelling Inventory

STATUS-OF-THE-CLASS

Students	Genre	Peer Conference	Revision	Teacher Edit	Final Draft	Teacher Observations

READING RESPONSE RUBRIC

Name: _____

    Book Title: _____

    Author: _____

Question:

	Does Not Meet	**Partially Meets**	**Meets**
Restatement			
Details from the Text to Support Thinking (at least three)			
Concluding Statement			
Stays on Topic			
Uses Proper Conventions			

Study-Group Resources

Writing

- *Mechanically Inclined: Building Grammar, Usage, and Style into Writer's Workshop* by Jeff Anderson
- *The Craft of Grammar: Integrated Instruction in Writer's Workshop* (DVD) by Jeff Anderson
- *Notebook Know-How: Strategies for the Writer's Notebook* by Aimee Buckner
- *Inside Notebooks: Bringing Out Writers, Grades 3–6* (VHS and DVD) by Aimee Buckner
- *Units of Study for Primary Writing: A Yearlong Curriculum* by Lucy Calkins
- *Boy Writers: Reclaiming Their Voices* by Ralph Fletcher
- *Craft Lessons: Teaching Writing K–8* by Ralph Fletcher and JoAnn Portalupi
- *Nonfiction Craft Lessons: Teaching Information Writing K–8* by Ralph Fletcher and JoAnn Portalupi
- *When Students Write* (VHS and DVD) by Ralph Fletcher and JoAnn Portalupi
- *The Revision Toolbox: Teaching Techniques That Work* by Georgia Heard
- *On Writing: A Memoir of the Craft* by Stephen King
- *When Writing Workshop Isn't Working: Answers to Ten Tough Questions, Grades 2–5* by Mark Overmeyer
- *Talking About Writing* (VHS and DVD) by Ralph Fletcher and JoAnn Portalupi
- *Study Driven: A Framework for Planning Units of Study in the Writing Workshop* by Katie Wood Ray
- *Wondrous Words: Writers and Writing in the Elementary Classroom* by Katie Wood Ray
- *Is That a Fact? Teaching Nonfiction Writing K–3* by Tony Stead
- *Time for Nonfiction* (VHS and DVD) by Tony Stead

Literature Discussions

- *Speak* (adolescent literature) by Laurie Anderson
- *Literature Circles: Voice and Choice in Book Clubs and Reading Groups* by Harvey Daniels

- *Looking into Literature* Circles (DVD) by Harvey Daniels
- *Comfort Me with Apples* (memoir) by Ruth Reichl
- *The Glass Castle: A Memoir* by Jeannette Walls
- *Keeping Katherine: A Mother's Journey to Acceptance* by Susan Zimmermann

Boys

- *Conferring with Boys* (DVD) by Max Brand
- *Boy Writers: Reclaiming Their Voices* by Ralph Fletcher
- *"Dude, Listen to This!" Engaging Boy Writers* (DVD) by Ralph Fletcher
- *Raising Cain: Protecting the Emotional Life of Boys* by Dan Kindlon and Michael Thompson
- *Real Boys: Rescuing Our Sons from the Myths of Boyhood* by William Pollack
- *Raising Cain: Exploring the Inner Lives of America's Boys* (DVD) by Michael Thompson

Reading

- *When Kids Can't Read: What Teachers Can Do, A Guide for Teachers 6–12* by Kylene Beers
- *Read, Write, and Talk* (VHS and DVD) by Stephanie Harvey and Anne Goudvis
- *Strategies that Work: Teaching Comprehension for Understanding and Engagement* by Stephanie Harvey and Anne Goudvis
- *Reading with Meaning: Teaching Comprehension in the Primary Grades* by Debbie Miller
- *Happy Reading! Creating a Predictable Structure for Joyful Teaching and Learning* (VHS and DVD) by Debbie Miller
- *Day-to-Day Assessment in the Reading Workshop: Making Informed Instructional Decisions in Grades 3–6* by Franki Sibberson and Karen Szymusiak
- *Beyond Leveled Books: Supporting Transitional Readers in Grades 2–5* by Franki Sibberson and Karen Szymusiak
- *Still Learning to Read: Teaching Students in Grades 3–6* by Franki Sibberson and Karen Szymusiak
- *Bringing Reading to Life: Instruction and Conversation, Grades 3–6* (VHS and DVD) by Franki Sibberson and Karen Szymusiak
- *Adventures in Graphica: Using Comics and Graphic Novels to Teach Comprehension, 2–6* by Terry Thompson

- *I Read It, but I Don't Get It: Comprehension Strategies for Adolescent Readers* by Cris Tovani
- *Thoughtful Reading: Teaching Comprehension to Adolescents* (VHS and DVD) by Cris Tovani

Struggling Readers

- *What Really Matters for Struggling Readers: Designing Research-Based Programs* by Richard L. Allington
- *A Classroom Teacher's Guide to Struggling Readers* by Curt Dudling-Marling and Patricia Paugh
- *Supporting Struggling Readers and Writers: Strategies for Classroom Intervention 3–6* by Dorothy S. Strickland, Kathy Ganske, and Joanne K. Monroe

Spelling and Word Study

- *Word Savvy: Integrating Vocabulary, Spelling, and Word Study, Grades 3–6* by Max Brand
- *A Day of Words: Integrating Word Work in the Intermediate Grades* (VHS and DVD) by Max Brand
- *Words Their Way: Word Study for Phonics, Vocabulary, and Spelling Instruction* by Donald R. Bear, Marcia Invernizzi, Shane R. Templeton, and Francine Johnston
- *Spelling K–8: Planning and Teaching* by Diane Snowball and Faye Bolton
- *Focus on Spelling* (VHS and DVD) by Diane Snowball

Fluency

- *Practical Fluency: Classroom Perspectives, Grades K–6* by Max Brand and Gayle Brand
- *The Fluent Reader: Oral Reading Strategies for Building Word Recognition, Fluency, and Comprehension* by Timothy V. Rasinski

Bibliography

Allen, Jennifer. 2006. *Becoming a Literacy Leader: Supporting Learning and Change.* Portland, ME: Stenhouse.

Allen, Jennifer, and Carolyn Bridges. 2008. *Literature Groups All Year Long* [DVD]. Portland, ME: Stenhouse.

Alliance for Excellent Education. 2004. "Tapping the Potential: Retaining and Developing High-Quality New Teachers." *Alliance for Excellent Education.* June 23. www.all4ed.org/files/TappingThePotential.pdf.

Andrade, Heidi. 2007/2008. "Self-Assessment Through Rubrics." *Educational Leadership* 65 (4): 60–63.

Atwell, Nancie. 1998. *In the Middle: New Understandings About Writing, Reading, and Learning.* 2nd ed. Portsmouth, NH: Heinemann.

Barth, Roland. 2006. "Improving Relationships Within the Schoolhouse." *Educational Leadership* 63 (6): 8–13.

Batten, Mary. 2002. *Hey, Daddy! Animal Fathers and Their Babies.* Atlanta, GA: Peachtree.

Black, Paul, and Dylan Wiliam. 1998. "Inside the Black Box: Raising Standards Through Classroom Assessment." *Phi Delta Kappan* 80 (2): 139–148. Available online at http://www.pdkintl.org/kappan/kbla9810.htm.

Blume, Judy. 2002. *Tales of a Fourth Grade Nothing.* New York: Scholastic.

Boreen, Jean, Mary K. Johnson, Donna Niday, and Joe Potts. 2000. *Mentoring Beginning Teachers: Guiding, Reflecting, Coaching.* Portland, ME: Stenhouse.

Boushey, Gail, and Joan Moser. 2006a. "Establishing an Environment for Learning." Available online at http:www.choiceliteracy.com/sistersdesignquestions.pdf.

———. 2006b. "Seven Steps: Designing the Physical Space." Available at http:www.choiceliteracy.com/sisters7final.pdf.

———. 2006c. *Simply Beautiful: Classroom Design for Gracious Living and Learning* [DVD]. Holden, ME: Choice Literacy Productions.

———. 2008. *Simply Organized: Classroom Libraries and Storage Areas* [DVD]. Holden, ME: Choice Literacy Productions.

Brookfield, Stephen D. 1995. *Becoming a Critically Reflective Teacher*. San Francisco: Jossey-Bass.

Buckner, Aimee. 2005. *Notebook Know-How: Strategies for the Writer's Notebook*. Portland, ME: Stenhouse.

———. 2009. *Notebook Connections: Strategies for the Reader's Notebook*. Portland, ME: Stenhouse.

Chappuis, Stephen, and Jan Chappuis. 2007/2008. "The Best Value in Formative Assessment." *Educational Leadership* 65 (4): 14–18.

Clements, Andrew. 1996. *Frindle*. New York: Aladdin.

———. 2001. *Jake Drake, Bully Buster*. New York: Aladdin.

Costa, Arthur L., and Robert J. Garmston. 1994. *Cognitive Coaching: A Foundation for Renaissance Schools*. Norwood, MA: Christopher-Gordon.

Daggett, Willard. 2008. Leading Successful Schools in Challenging Times. Presentation at the Maine Principals' Association, November, Portland, ME.

Dahl, Roald. 2007. *Fantastic Mr. Fox*. New York: Puffin Books.

Daniels, Harvey. 2001. *Looking into Literature Circles* [DVD]. Portland, ME: Stenhouse.

Dudley-Marling, Curt, and Patricia C. Paugh. 2004. *A Classroom Teacher's Guide to Struggling Readers*. Portsmouth, NH: Heinemann.

Elbow, Peter. 1973. *Writing Without Teachers*. New York: Oxford University Press.

El Nabli, Dina. 2006. *Eleanor Roosevelt: First Lady of the World*. Time for Kids Biographies. New York: HarperCollins.

Fendler, Donn. 1992. *Lost on a Mountain in Maine*. New York: Beech Tree Books.

Fletcher, Ralph. 2000. *Grandpa Never Lies*. New York: Clarion.

———. 2005. *Marshfield Dreams: When I Was a Kid*. New York: Henry Holt.

———. 2006. *Boy Writers: Reclaiming Their Voices*. Portland, ME: Stenhouse.

———. 2007. *How to Write Your Life Story.* New York: HarperCollins.

———. 2008. *"Dude, Listen to This!" Engaging Boy Writers* [DVD]. Portland, ME: Stenhouse.

Fletcher, Ralph, and JoAnn Portalupi. 2001. *Nonfiction Craft Lessons: Teaching Information Writing K–8.* Portland, ME: Stenhouse.

Fullan, Michael. 2001. *Leading in a Culture of Change.* San Francisco: Jossey-Bass.

Gannett, Ruth Stiles. 2005. *My Father's Dragon.* New York: Yearling.

Gantos, Jack. 2005. "The Follower." In *Guys Write for Guys Read,* ed. Jon Scieszka. New York: Scholastic.

Glasser, William. 1990. *The Quality School: Managing Students Without Coercion.* New York: Harper and Row.

Graves, Donald H. 2001. *The Energy to Teach.* Portsmouth, NH: Heinemann.

Halliday, Michael A. K. 1993. "Towards a Language-Based Theory of Learning." *Linguistics and Education* 5 (2): 93–116.

Harvey, Stephanie, and Anne Goudvis. 2007. *Strategies That Work: Teaching Comprehension for Understanding and Engagement.* 2nd ed. Portland, ME: Stenhouse.

Heard, Georgia. 2002. *The Revision Toolbox: Teaching Techniques That Work.* Portsmouth, NH: Heinemann.

Hindley, Joanne. 1996. *In the Company of Children.* Portland, ME: Stenhouse.

Horde, Shirley M., and William A. Sommers. 2008. *Leading Professional Learning Communities: Voices from Research and Practice.* Thousand Oaks, CA: Corwin.

Hunter, Madeline. 1982. *Mastery Teaching.* El Segundo, CA: TIP Publications.

Hurwitz, Johanna. 1988. *Class Clown.* New York: Scholastic.

Johnson, Susan, Sarah Birkeland, Susan Kardos, David Kauffman, Edward Liu, and Heather Peske. 2001. "Retaining the Next Generation of Teachers: The Importance of School-Based Support." *Harvard Education Letter* 17 (4): 4. Available online at http://www.edletter.org/past/issues/2001-ja/support.shtml.

Johnson, Thomas, ed. (1976). *The Complete Poems of Emily Dickinson.* Boston: Back Bay Books.

Johnston, Peter H. 2004. *Choice Words: How Language Affects Children's Learning.* Portland, ME: Stenhouse.

Kendall, Juli. 2007. "Three Simple Secrets of School-Based Coaching." *Journal of Staff Development* 28 (1): 76.

King, Stephen. 2000. *On Writing: A Memoir of the Craft*. New York: Scribner.

Laminack, Lester. 2004. *Saturdays and Teacakes*. Atlanta, GA: Peachtree.

Long, Susi, Ami Abramson, April Boone, Carly Borchelt, Robbie Kalish, Erin Miller, Julie Parks, and Carmen Tisdale. 2006. *Tensions and Triumphs in the Early Years of Teaching: Real-World Findings and Advice for Supporting New Teachers*. Urbana, IL: National Council of Teachers of English.

Martineau, Pamela. 2007. "Tapping Instant Messaging." *Education Week's Digital Directions* 1 (Fall): 10. Available online at http://www.edweek.org/dd/articles/2007/09/12/02im.h01.html.

Marzano, Robert. 2003. *What Works in Schools: Translating Research into Action*. Alexandria, VA: Association for Supervision and Curriculum Development.

Maslow, Abraham. 1943. "A Theory of Human Motivation." *Psychological Review* 50: 370–396. Available online at http://pychclassics.yorku.ca/Maslow/motivation.htm.

McDonald, Megan. 2005. *Stink: The Incredible Shrinking Kid*. Cambridge, MA: Candlewick.

Miller, Debbie. 2002. *Reading with Meaning: Teaching Comprehension in the Primary Grades*. Portland, ME: Stenhouse.

———. 2008. *Teaching with Intention: Defining Beliefs, Aligning Practice, Taking Action, K–5*. Portland, ME: Stenhouse.

Moir, Ellen. 2005. "Launching the Next Generation of Teachers: The New Teacher Center's Model for Quality Induction and Mentoring." In *Teacher Mentoring and Induction: The State of the Art and Beyond*, ed. Hal Portner. Thousand Oaks, CA: Corwin.

———. 2008. "Policy Focus Impacts Teacher Induction." *New Teacher Center Reflections* X (1): 1, 13. Available online at http://www.newteachercenter.org/newsletters/ReflectionsW08.pdf.

Morgan, Bruce, Debbie Miller, and Ellin Keene. 2007. Presentation given at the National Council of Teachers of English annual convention, November, New York.

Naylor, Phyllis Reynolds. 1996. *The Fear Place*. New York: Aladdin.

New Teacher Center. 2006. NTC Policy Paper. *Understanding New York City's Groundbreaking Induction Initiative: Policy Implications for Local, State, and National Education Leaders*. www.newteachercenter.org/pdfs/NYCPolicyPaper.pdf.

Nye, Naomi Shihab. 1994. *Red Suitcase (American Poets Continuum)*. Brockport, NY: BOA Editions.

Pallotta, Jerry. 2000. *Dory Story*. Watertown, MA: Charlesbridge.

Patrick, Denise Lewis. 2005. *Jackie Robinson: Strong Inside and Out*. Time for Kids Biographies. New York: HarperCollins.

Pearson, P. David, and M. C. Gallagher. 1983. "Instruction of Reading Comprehension." *Contemporary Educational Psychology* 8: 319–344.

Pinnell Gay Su, and Emily Rodgers. 2004. "Reflective Inquiry as a Tool for Professional Development." In *Improving Reading Achievement Through Professional Development*, eds. Dorothy Strickland and Michael Kamil. Norwood, MA: Christopher-Gordon.

Plourde, Lynn. 2008. *Margaret Chase Smith: A Woman for President*. Watertown, MA: Charlesbridge.

Polacco, Patricia. 2001. *The Keeping Quilt*. New York: Aladdin.

Rogers, Carl. 1983. *Freedom to Learn for the 80s*. Columbus, OH: Charles E. Merrill.

Rylant, Cynthia. 1995. *Mr. Putter and Tabby Pick the Pears*. New York: Scholastic.

Sachar, Louis. 1985. *Sideways Stories from Wayside School*. New York: HarperCollins.

Satterfield, Kathryn Hoffman. 2005. *Benjamin Franklin: A Man of Many Talents*. Time for Kids Biographies. New York: HarperCollins.

Scieszka, Jon, ed. 2005. *Guys Write for Guys Read*. New York: Scholastic.

Sibberson, Franki, and Karen Szymusiak. 2003. *Still Learning to Read: Teaching Students in Grades 3–6*. Portland, ME: Stenhouse.

———. 2004. *Bringing Reading to Life: Instruction and Conversations, Grades 3–6 [DVD]*. Portland, ME: Stenhouse.

———. 2008. *Day-to Day-Assessment in the Reading Workshop: Making Informed Instructional Decisions in Grades 3–6*. New York: Scholastic.

Siebold, Jan. 2002. *Doing Time Online*. Morton Grove, IL: Albert Whitman.

Skelton, Renee. 2005. *Harriet Tubman: A Woman of Courage*. Time for Kids Biographies. New York: HarperCollins.

Sweeney, Diane. 2003. *Learning Along the Way: Professional Development by and for Teachers*. Portland, ME: Stenhouse.

Szymusiak, Karen, and Franki Sibberson. 2001. *Beyond Leveled Books: Supporting Transitional Readers in Grades 2–5*. Portland, ME: Stenhouse.

ThinkExist.com. Dorothy Neville quote. Retrieved June 16, 2009, from http://thinkexist.com/quotation/the_real_art_of_conversation_is_not_only_to_say/10625.html.

Thompson, Terry. 2008. *Adventures in Graphica: Using Comics and Graphic Novels to Teach Comprehension,* 2–6. Portland, ME: Stenhouse.

Tomlinson, Carol Ann. 2007/2008. "Learning to Love Assessment." *Educational Leadership* 65 (4): 8–13.

Tomlinson, Carol Ann, and Jay McTighe. 2006. *Integrating Differentiated Instruction and Understanding by Design.* Alexandria, VA: Association for Supervision and Curriculum Development.

Van Allsburg, Chris. 1990. *Just a Dream.* Boston: Houghton Mifflin.

———. 1999. *The Wretched Stone.* Boston: Houghton Mifflin.

Vygotsky, L. S. 1978. *Mind in Society: The Development of Higher Psychological Processes.* Cambridge, MA: Harvard University Press.

Walls, Jeanette. 2005. *The Glass Castle: A Memoir.* New York: Scribner.

Watt, Melanie. 2006. *Scaredy Squirrel.* Tonawanda, NY: Kids Can Press.

———. 2007. *Chester.* Tonawanda, NY: Kids Can Press.

Wiebke, Kathy, and Joe Bardin. 2009. "New Teacher Support: A Comprehensive Induction Program Can Increase Teacher Retention and Improve Performance." *Journal of Staff Development* 30 (1): 34–38.

Wiliam, Dylan. 2007/2008. "Changing Classroom Practice." *Educational Leadership* 65 (4): 36–42.

Wong, Harry K. 2005. "New Teacher Induction: The Foundation for Comprehensive, Coherent, and Sustained Professional Development." In *Teacher Mentoring and Induction: The State of the Art and Beyond,* ed. Hal Portner. Thousand Oaks, CA: Corwin.

Zimmermann, Susan. 2004. *Keeping Katherine: A Mother's Journey to Acceptance.* New York: Three Rivers Press.